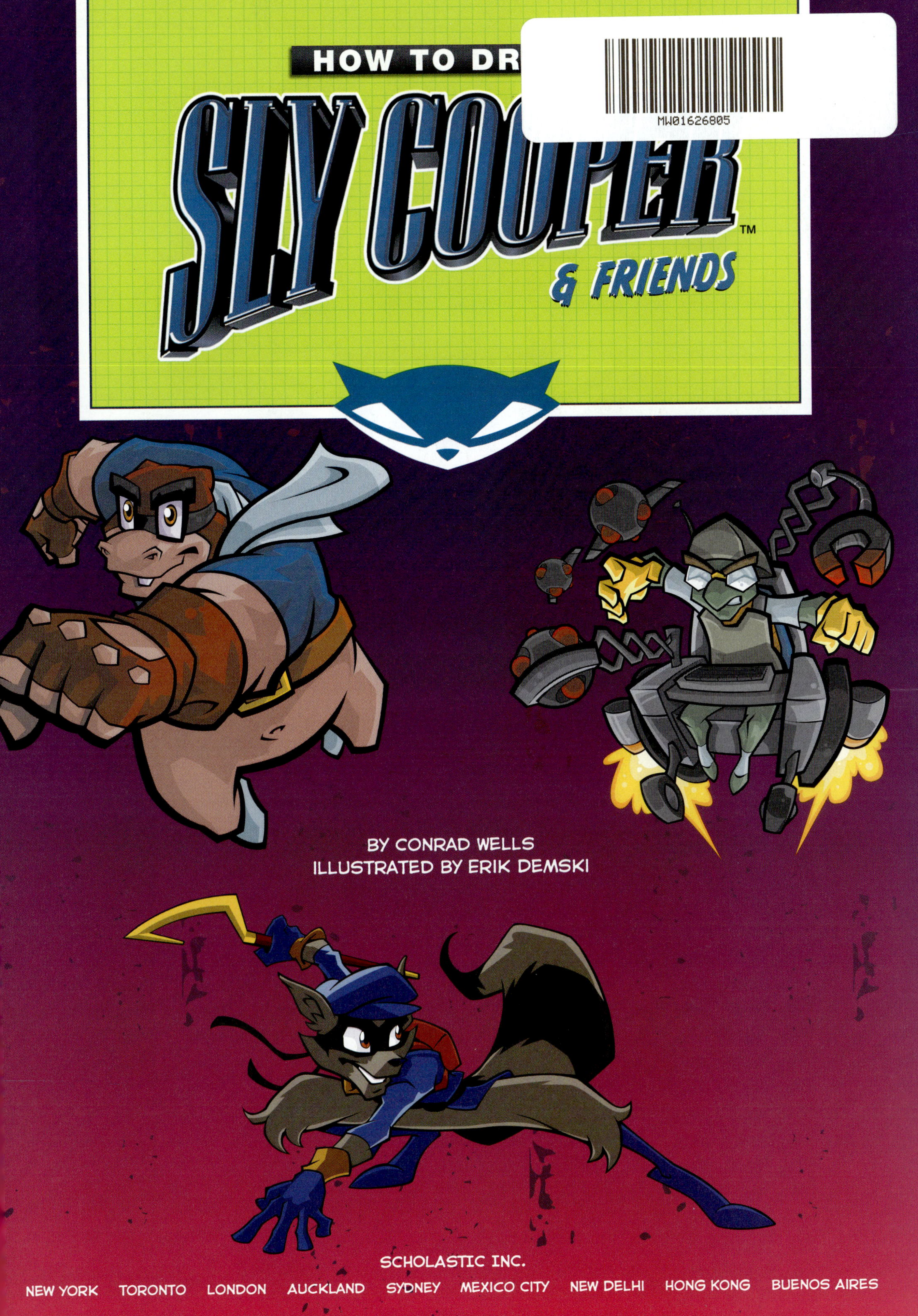

BY CONRAD WELLS
ILLUSTRATED BY ERIK DEMSKI

SCHOLASTIC INC.
NEW YORK TORONTO LONDON AUCKLAND SYDNEY MEXICO CITY NEW DELHI HONG KONG BUENOS AIRES

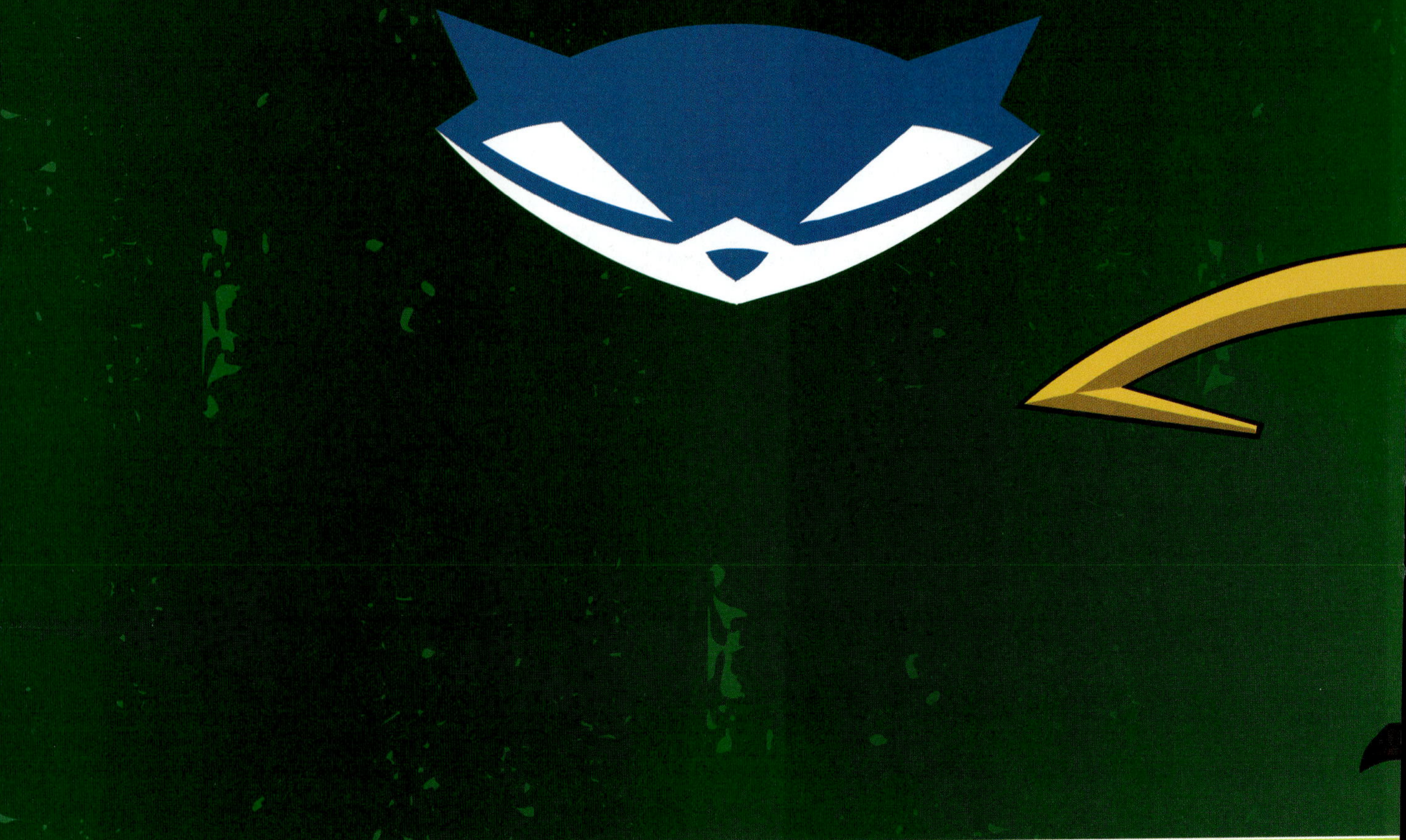

ISBN 0-439-82946-1

Published by Scholastic Inc.

12 11 10 9 8 7 6 5 4 3 2 1 6 7 8 9 10/

Printed in the U.S.A.
First printing, January 2006

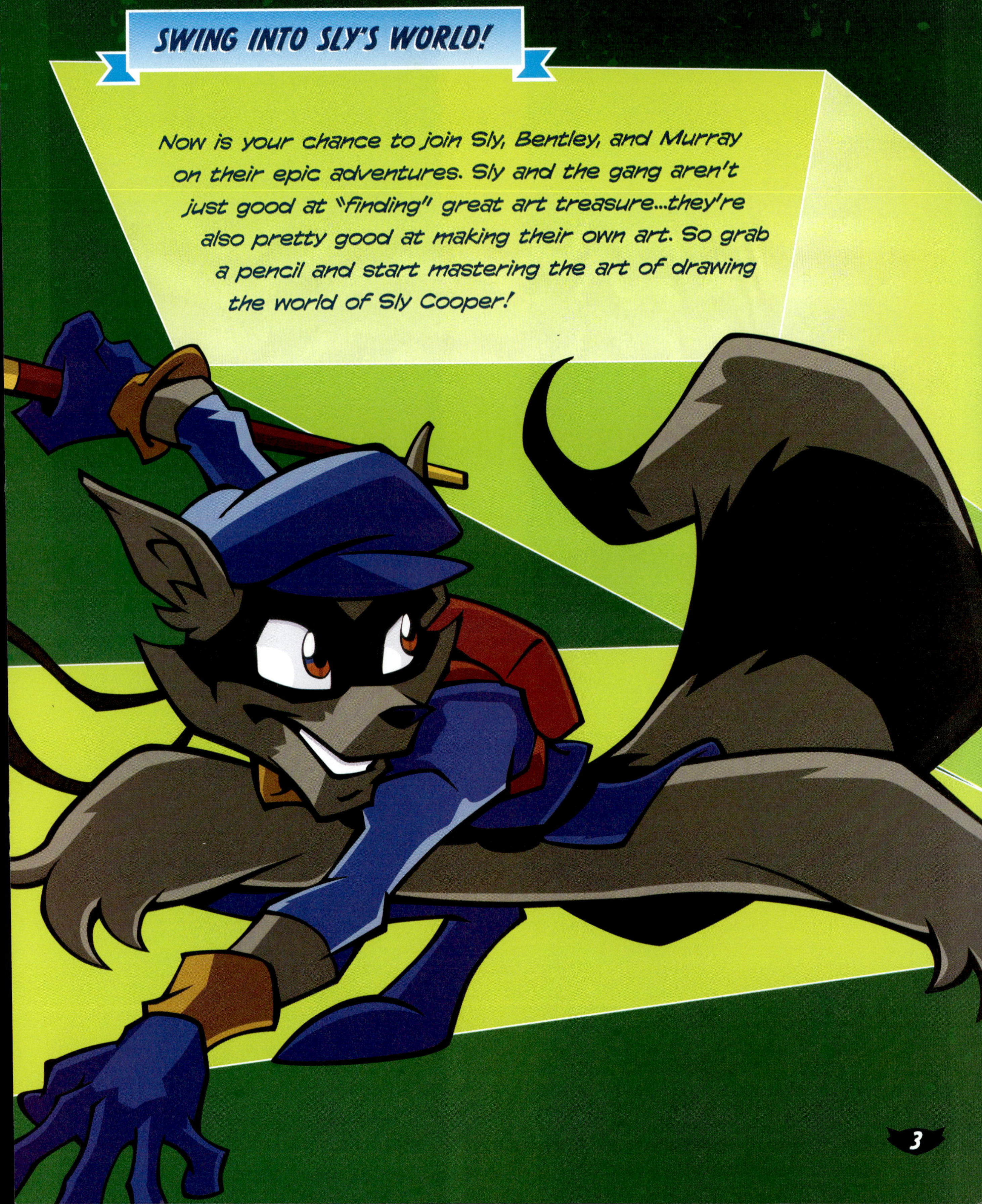

SWING INTO SLY'S WORLD!

Now is your chance to join Sly, Bentley, and Murray on their epic adventures. Sly and the gang aren't just good at "finding" great art treasure...they're also pretty good at making their own art. So grab a pencil and start mastering the art of drawing the world of Sly Cooper!

THINGS YOU WILL NEED:

- A pencil
- Clean, blank paper
- A fresh, new eraser

THINGS YOU MIGHT NEED:

- Graph paper
- A black pen
- Markers, color pencils, and/or crayons
- Water-based paint
- A small (thin) paintbrush
- Scrap paper (for practice)
- Gel pens

WORD FROM THE RACCOONUS:

Keep your eyes open for the Thievius Raccoonus. When you see the icon below, one of the Cooper family drawing secrets is sure to follow!

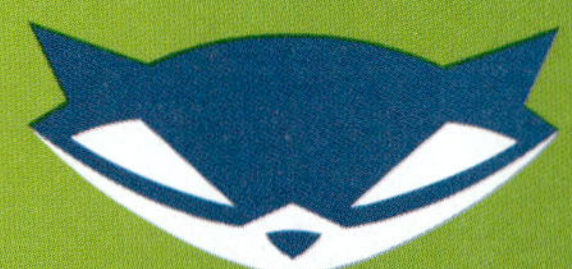

GETTING STARTED

The first step to doing the drawings in this book is to "shape up" the drawing. When you shape up a drawing, you break it down into one of five basic shapes—circles, ovals, squares, rectangles, and triangles. Take a little time now to practice these basic shapes. Just take out a sheet of scrap paper and fill it up. This is a great way to loosen up and get ready to draw!

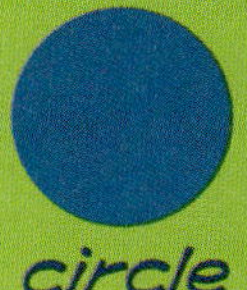
circle

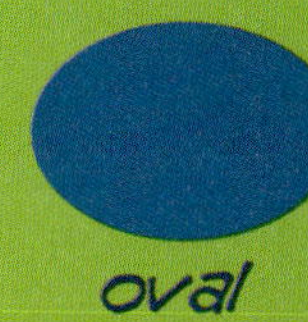
oval

square

rectangle

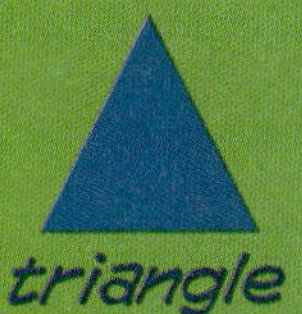
triangle

A FEW THINGS TO REMEMBER

- *Using the basic shapes to create drawings is not always as easy as it looks. Don't get discouraged if you're not happy with your drawings at first. Just keep practicing—It's the only way to get better!*
- *Don't try to be perfect! If you make a mistake, don't worry. Not even professional artists get everything right the first time. Just be patient and have fun!*
- *Always start your drawing in the middle of the paper. That way you won't run out of room before you are done.*

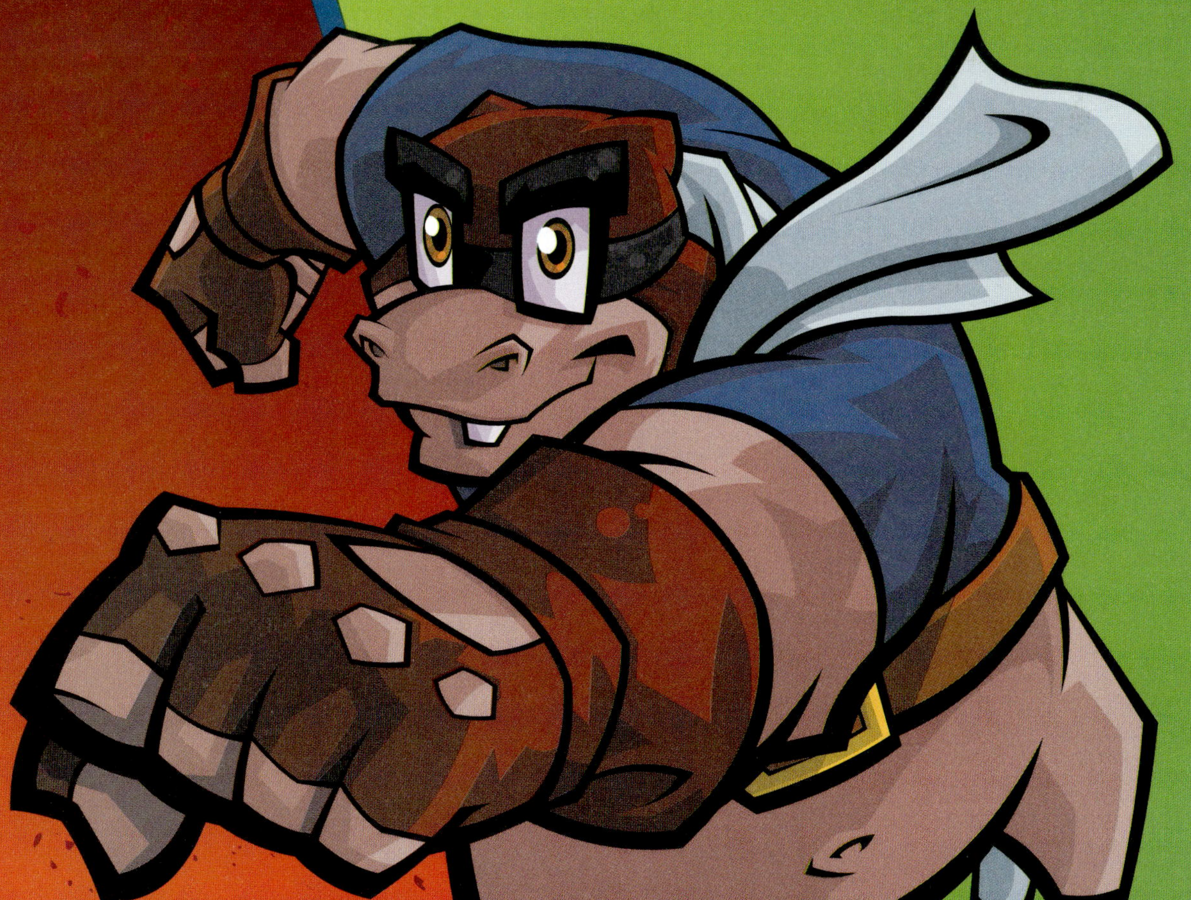

SLY COOPER

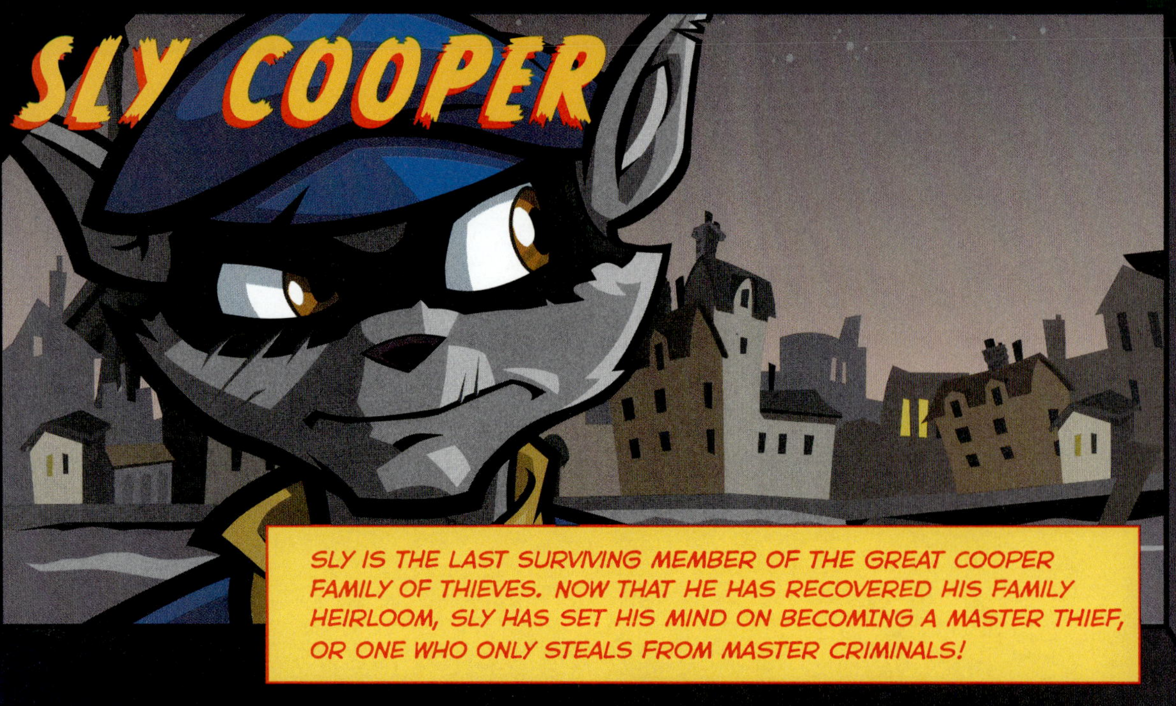

SLY IS THE LAST SURVIVING MEMBER OF THE GREAT COOPER FAMILY OF THIEVES. NOW THAT HE HAS RECOVERED HIS FAMILY HEIRLOOM, SLY HAS SET HIS MIND ON BECOMING A MASTER THIEF, OR ONE WHO ONLY STEALS FROM MASTER CRIMINALS!

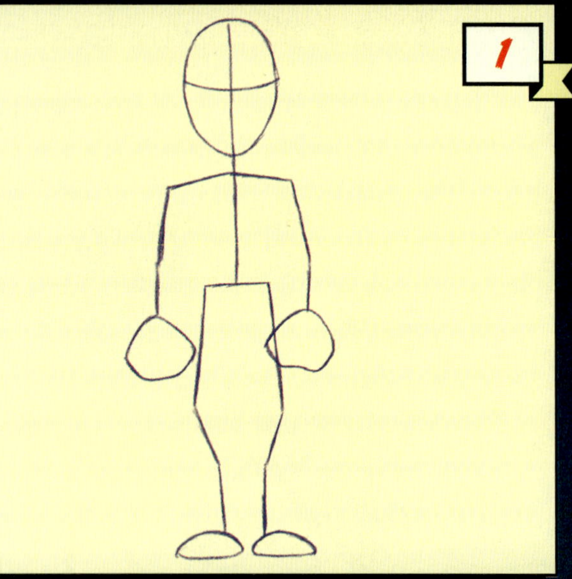

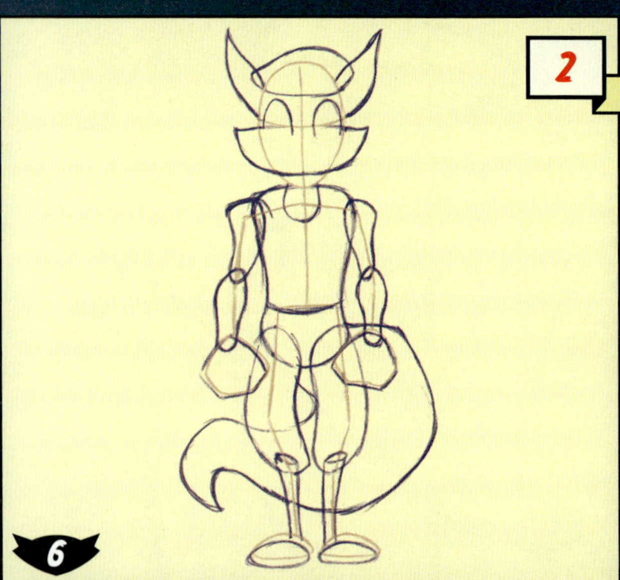

1. Begin with a basic stick figure with ovals for the head, feet, and hands. When you're happy with the shape of your drawing, move on to the next step.

2. Now use the other basic shapes you learned to create the outline for Sly's body. Here's a hint—use curves to create Sly's ringed raccoon tail!

3. When that's done, start adding some basic details. Take your time and remember to use a light line. For now, use a pencil to color in Sly's mask. And don't forget to add a little more detail to his gloves as well.

4. Now concentrate on Sly's tail, pants, and legs. Don't forget the tiny zigzag lines on his tail. This detail will bring out the texture of Sly's fur.

5. Erase any lines you don't need and darken the lines you want to keep. Paying close attention to the small details (such as the design on Sly's belt buckle) is one of the keys to artistic success.

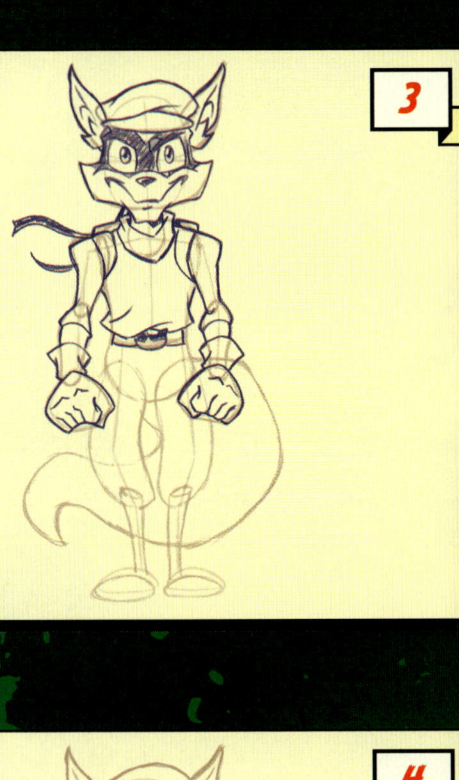

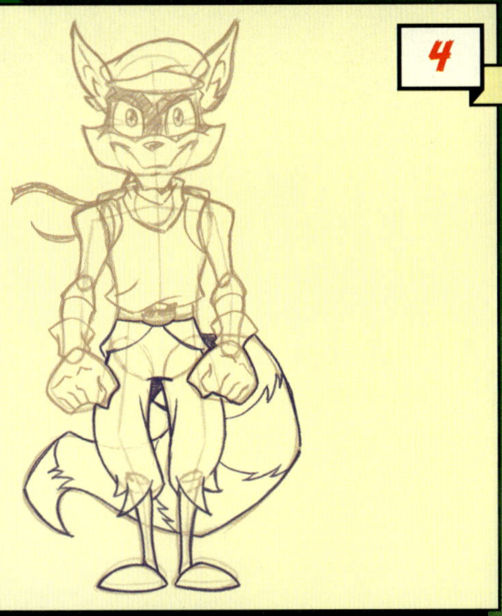

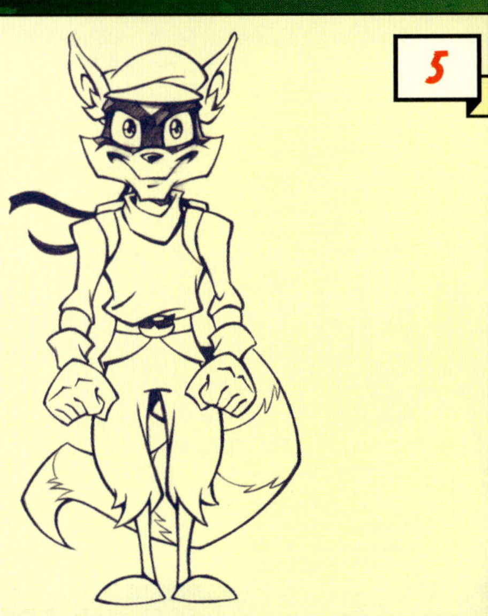

THE BIG FINISH

Time to add a little color! Gray and black work well for his tail, and black will make his mask blend into the dark of night. Don't forget to add shading to bring Sly to life.

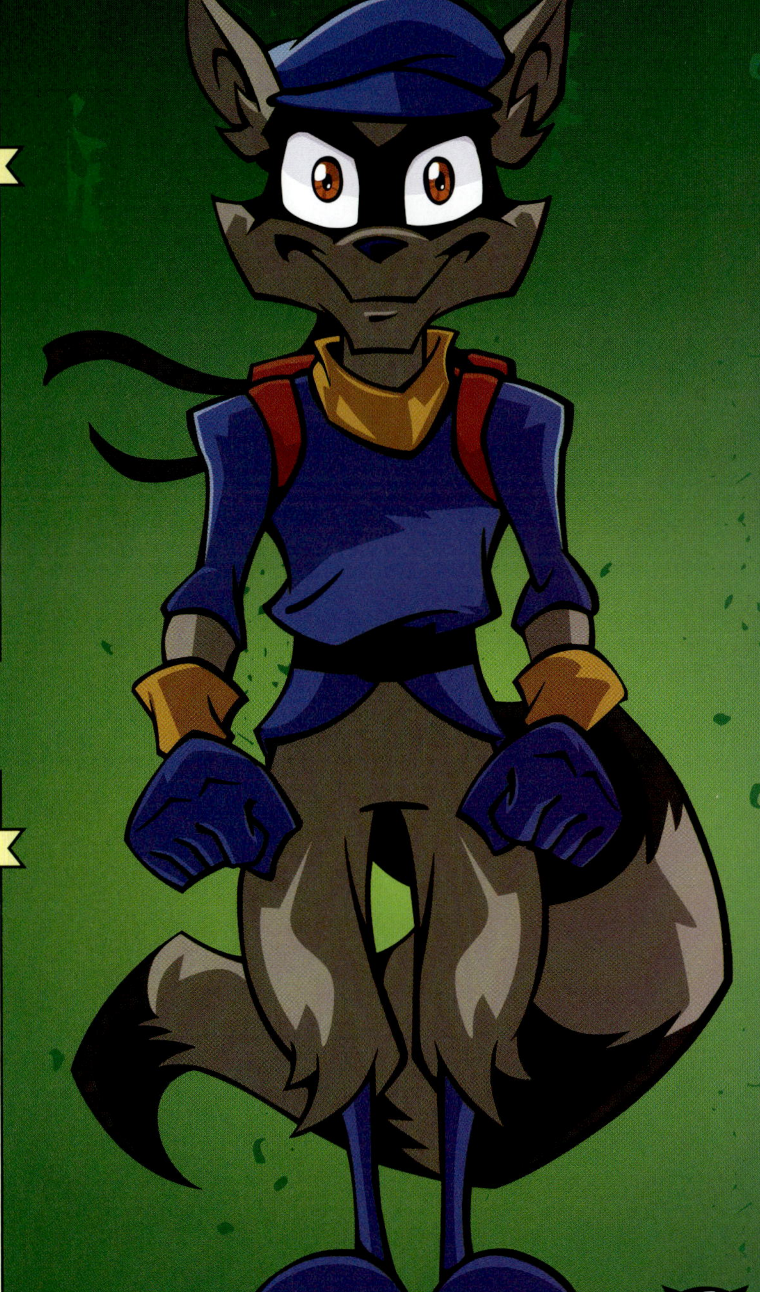

BENTLEY

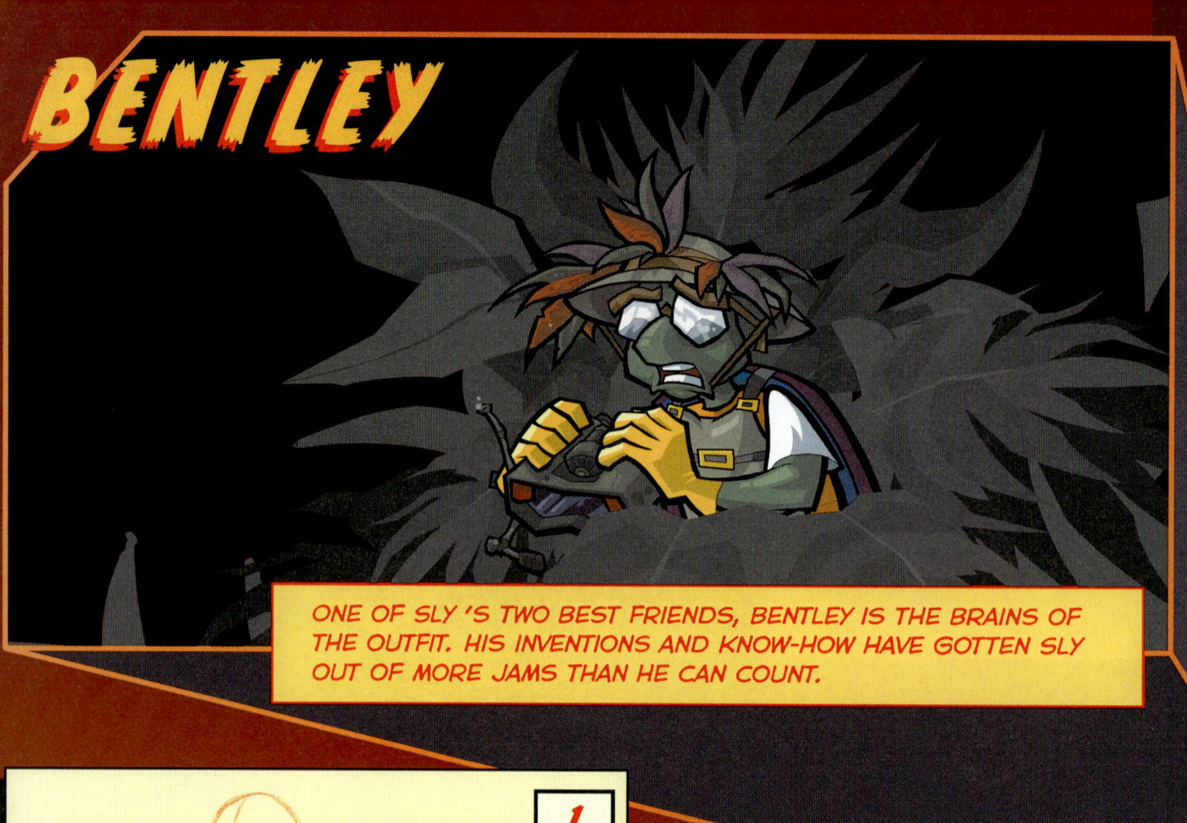

ONE OF SLY'S TWO BEST FRIENDS, BENTLEY IS THE BRAINS OF THE OUTFIT. HIS INVENTIONS AND KNOW-HOW HAVE GOTTEN SLY OUT OF MORE JAMS THAN HE CAN COUNT.

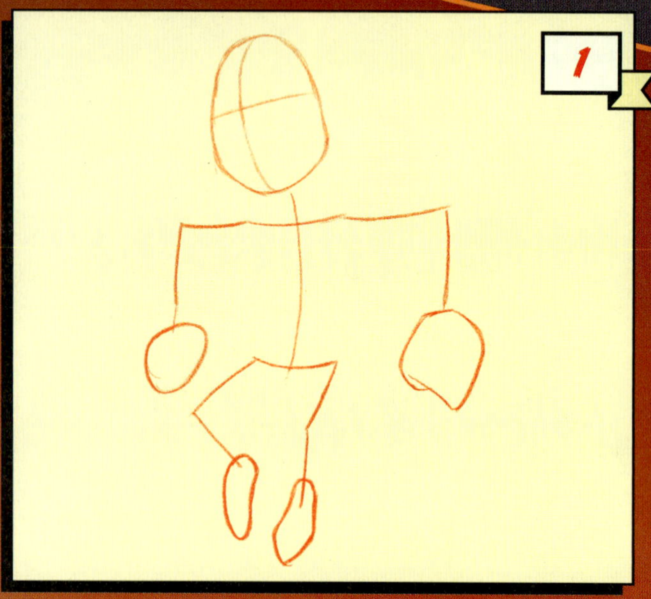

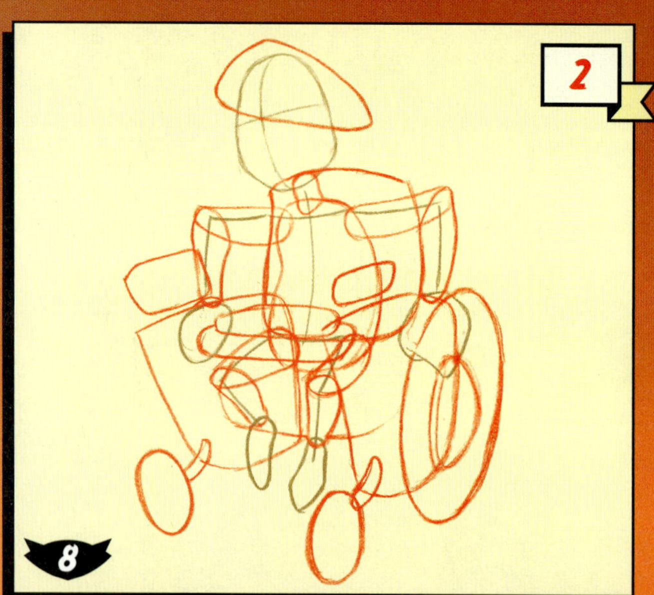

1. Start with a basic stick figure for Bentley's body and an oval for his head, hands, and feet.
2. Shape Bentley up by adding circles and squares to create his body and limbs. Don't forget to add the ovals for Bentley's helmet and chair wheels.
3. Add Bentley's "tortoiseshell glasses," safety helmet, and other basic details to the top half of the drawing.
4. As a great inventor, Bentley never goes far without some sort of gadget or high-tech gear. Be sure to add detail and strengthen the lines of his laptop, PDA, and wheels.
5. Grab a dark-colored marker and retrace the lines you like. Erase the lines that don't fit anymore.

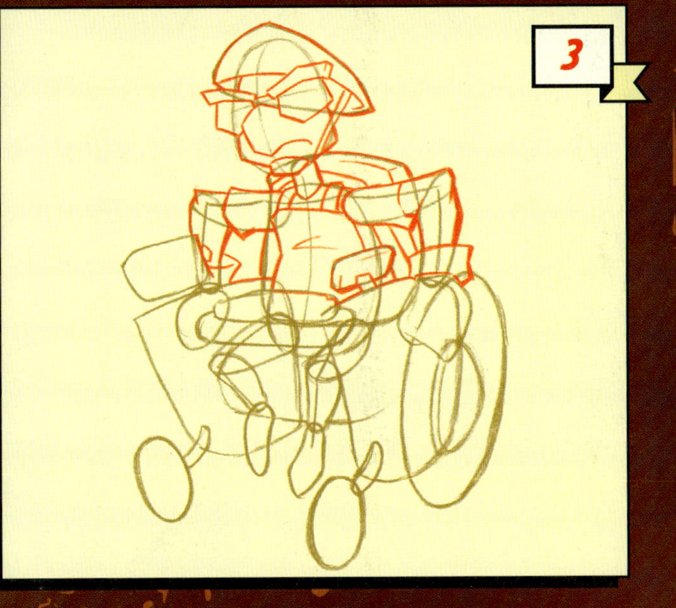

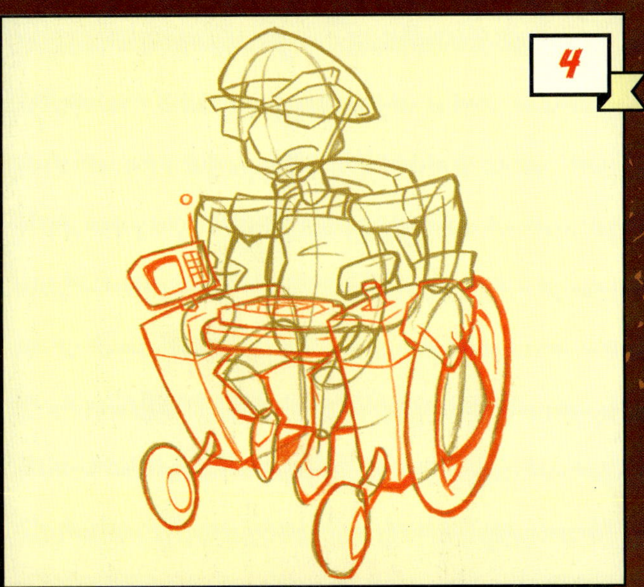

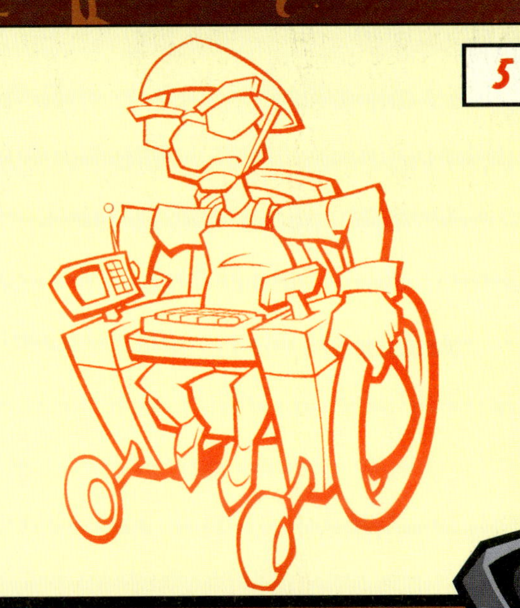

THE BIG FINISH

Time to bring out the color! Pay special attention to Bentley's bright yellow gloves, and add some highlights to create some depth and dimension.

MURRAY

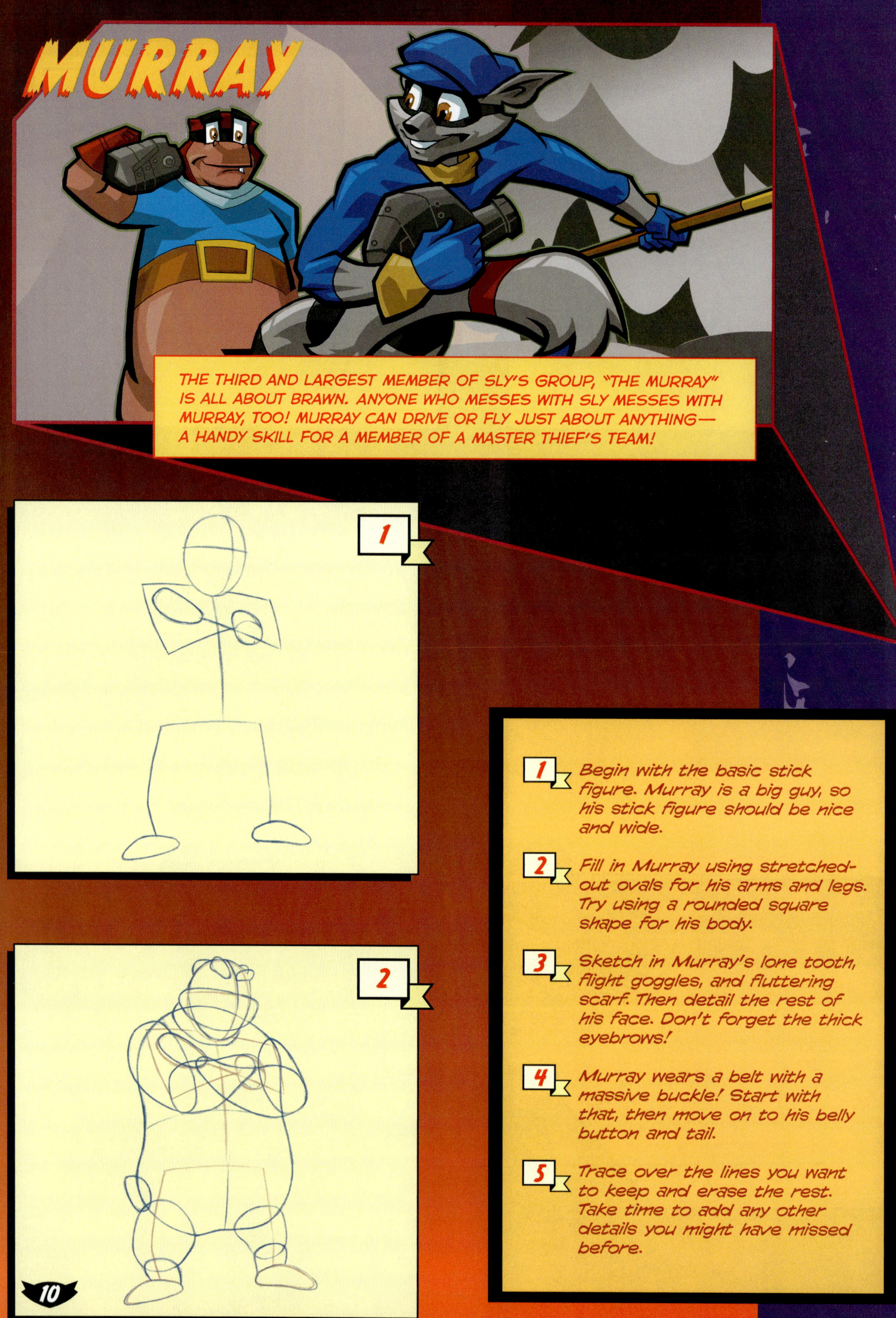

THE THIRD AND LARGEST MEMBER OF SLY'S GROUP, "THE MURRAY" IS ALL ABOUT BRAWN. ANYONE WHO MESSES WITH SLY MESSES WITH MURRAY, TOO! MURRAY CAN DRIVE OR FLY JUST ABOUT ANYTHING—A HANDY SKILL FOR A MEMBER OF A MASTER THIEF'S TEAM!

1. Begin with the basic stick figure. Murray is a big guy, so his stick figure should be nice and wide.
2. Fill in Murray using stretched-out ovals for his arms and legs. Try using a rounded square shape for his body.
3. Sketch in Murray's lone tooth, flight goggles, and fluttering scarf. Then detail the rest of his face. Don't forget the thick eyebrows!
4. Murray wears a belt with a massive buckle! Start with that, then move on to his belly button and tail.
5. Trace over the lines you want to keep and erase the rest. Take time to add any other details you might have missed before.

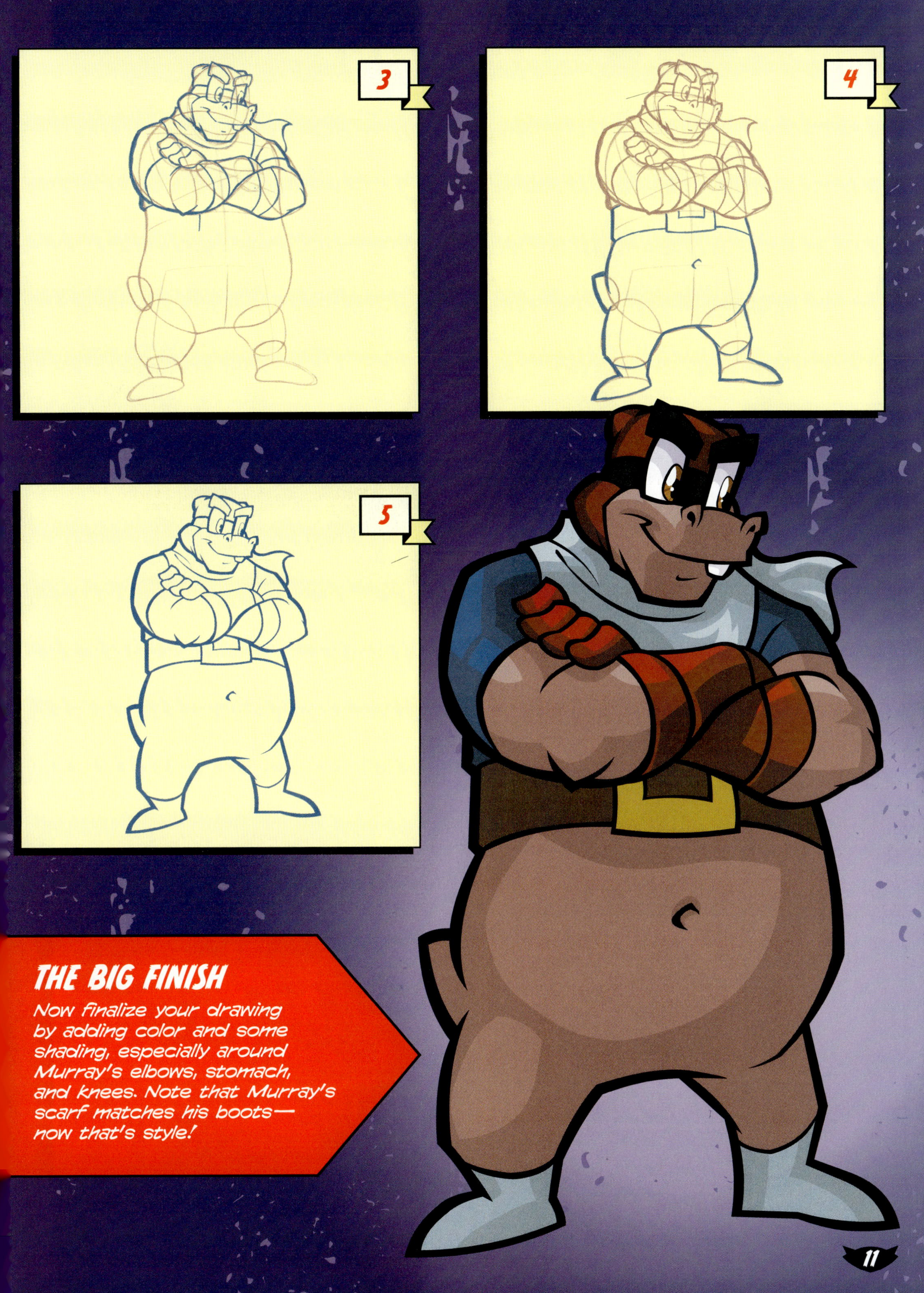

THE BIG FINISH

Now finalize your drawing by adding color and some shading, especially around Murray's elbows, stomach, and knees. Note that Murray's scarf matches his boots—now that's style!

INSPECTOR CARMELITA MONTOYA FOX

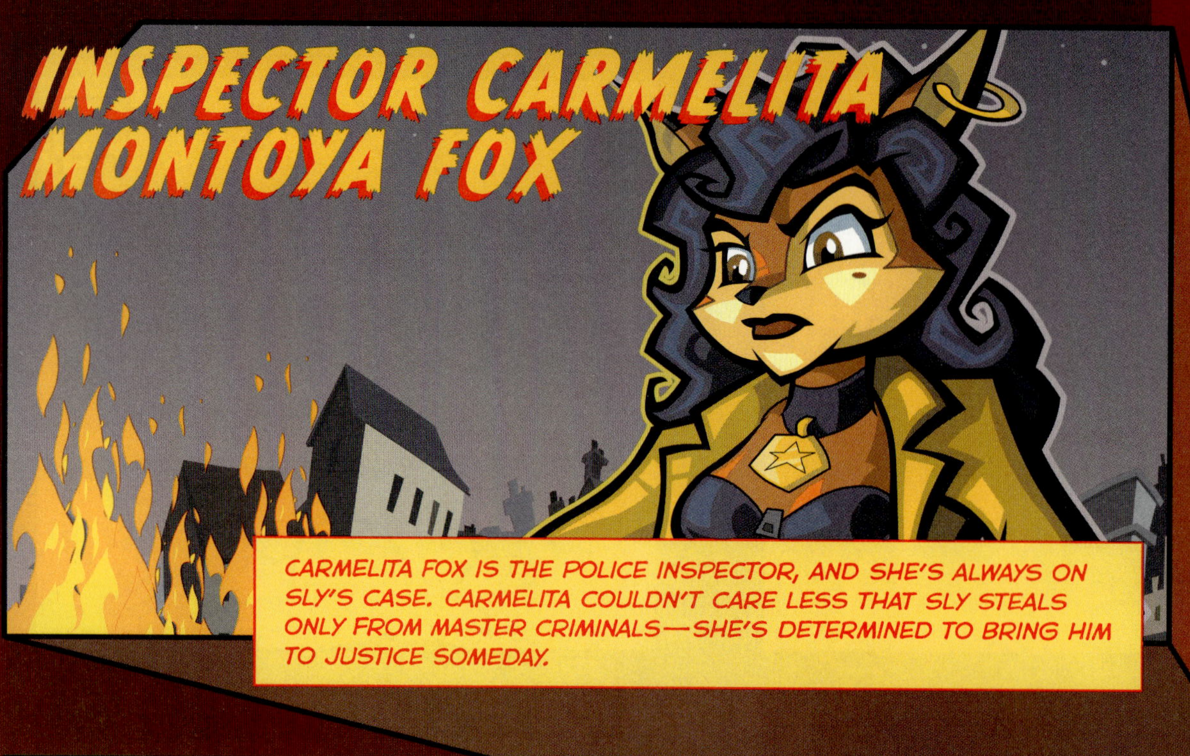

CARMELITA FOX IS THE POLICE INSPECTOR, AND SHE'S ALWAYS ON SLY'S CASE. CARMELITA COULDN'T CARE LESS THAT SLY STEALS ONLY FROM MASTER CRIMINALS—SHE'S DETERMINED TO BRING HIM TO JUSTICE SOMEDAY.

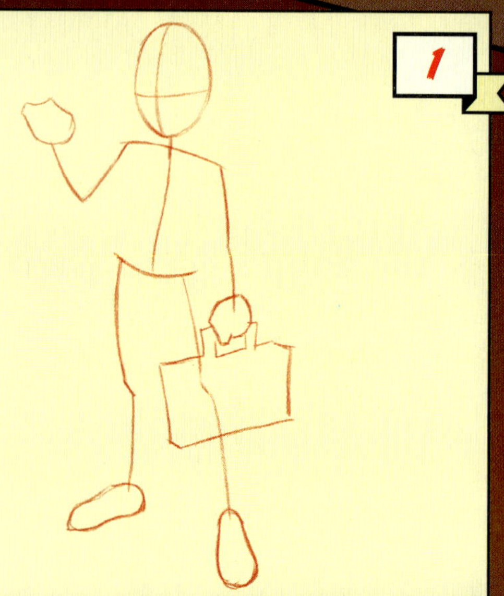

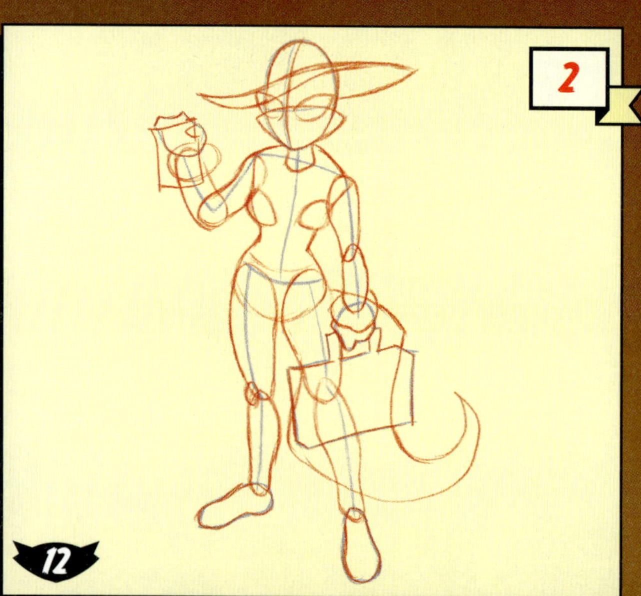

1. Begin with the basic shapes you've been practicing: circles, ovals, and a stick-figure body. Add the rough outline of a three-dimensional rectangle with a handle. This will become Inspector Fox's detective briefcase later.

2. Fill in Inspector Fox's basic shape. Use two semicircles to create her tail and the rim of her wide-brimmed hat.

3. Time to add the first wave of details. You'll need to use lots of small semicircles to create her hair and cool shades.

4. Add some details to Inspector Fox's boots and strengthen the lines of her tail. And don't forget to add the heel of her right boot!

5. Darken the lines you want to keep by going over them again with a marker or a dark colored pencil. Erase the stray lines and anything else that doesn't fit with your final sketch.

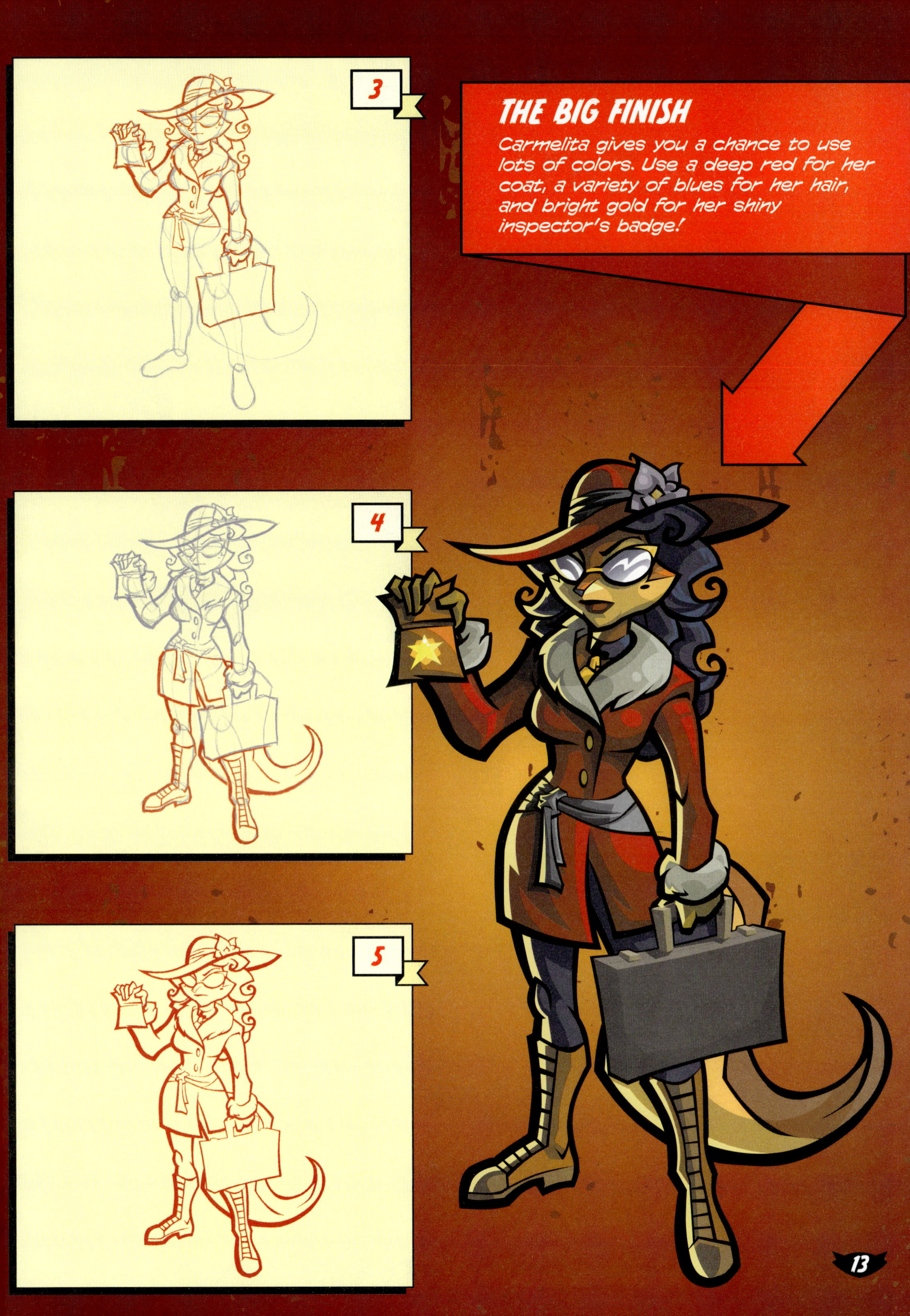

THE BIG FINISH

Carmelita gives you a chance to use lots of colors. Use a deep red for her coat, a variety of blues for her hair, and bright gold for her shiny inspector's badge!

SLY, READY FOR ACTION

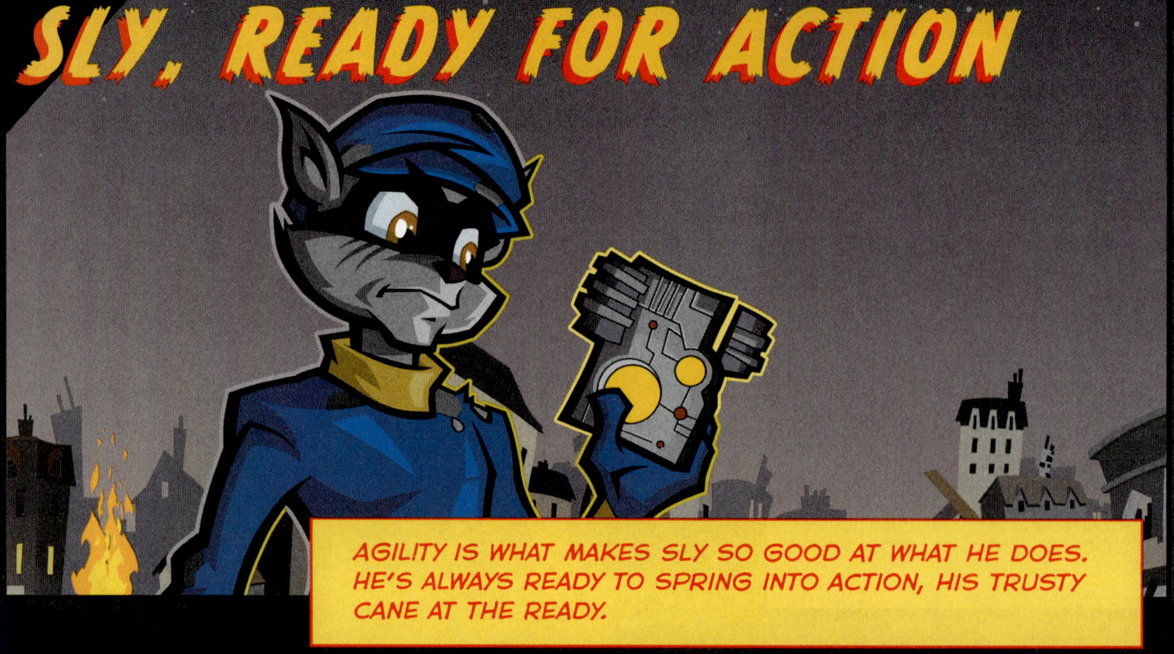

AGILITY IS WHAT MAKES SLY SO GOOD AT WHAT HE DOES. HE'S ALWAYS READY TO SPRING INTO ACTION, HIS TRUSTY CANE AT THE READY.

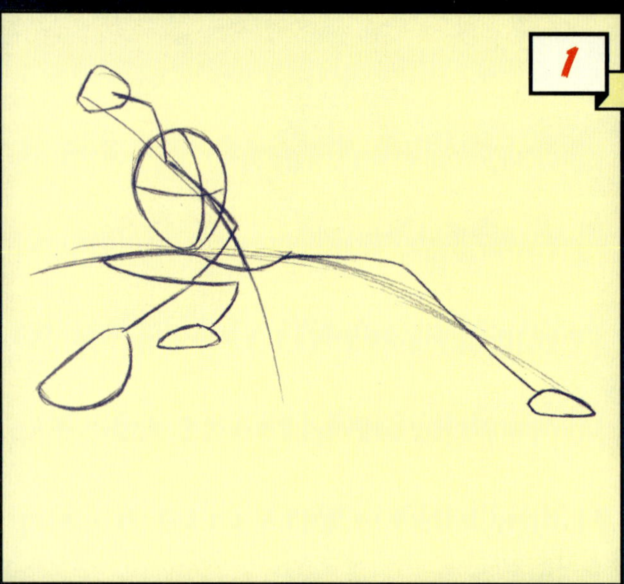

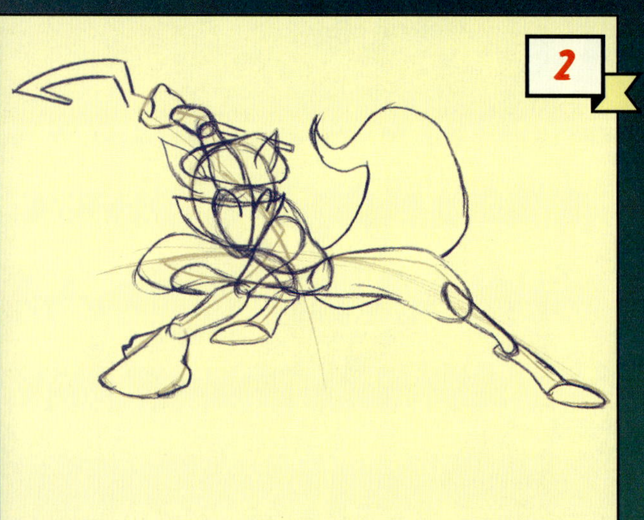

1. Time for some action! Start Sly off with a stick figure, then stretch it out. Sly's right leg should be bent in a crouch, while his left leg is extended.
2. Give Sly a body by adding some basic shapes to fill him out. Don't forget the smaller details like Sly's cane, ears, and the beginnings of his cap!
3. Carefully sketch Sly's fingers, taking your time and focusing on the details in his knuckles and thumb. Then start adding details to Sly's clothes.
4. Detail the bottom half of your drawing. Add the frayed bottom of Sly's pants for authenticity, and don't forget the zigzagging fur lines on his tail.
5. Clean up your drawing. If you'd like, this is your chance to add a final layer of detail, such as action or movement lines for Sly's cane.

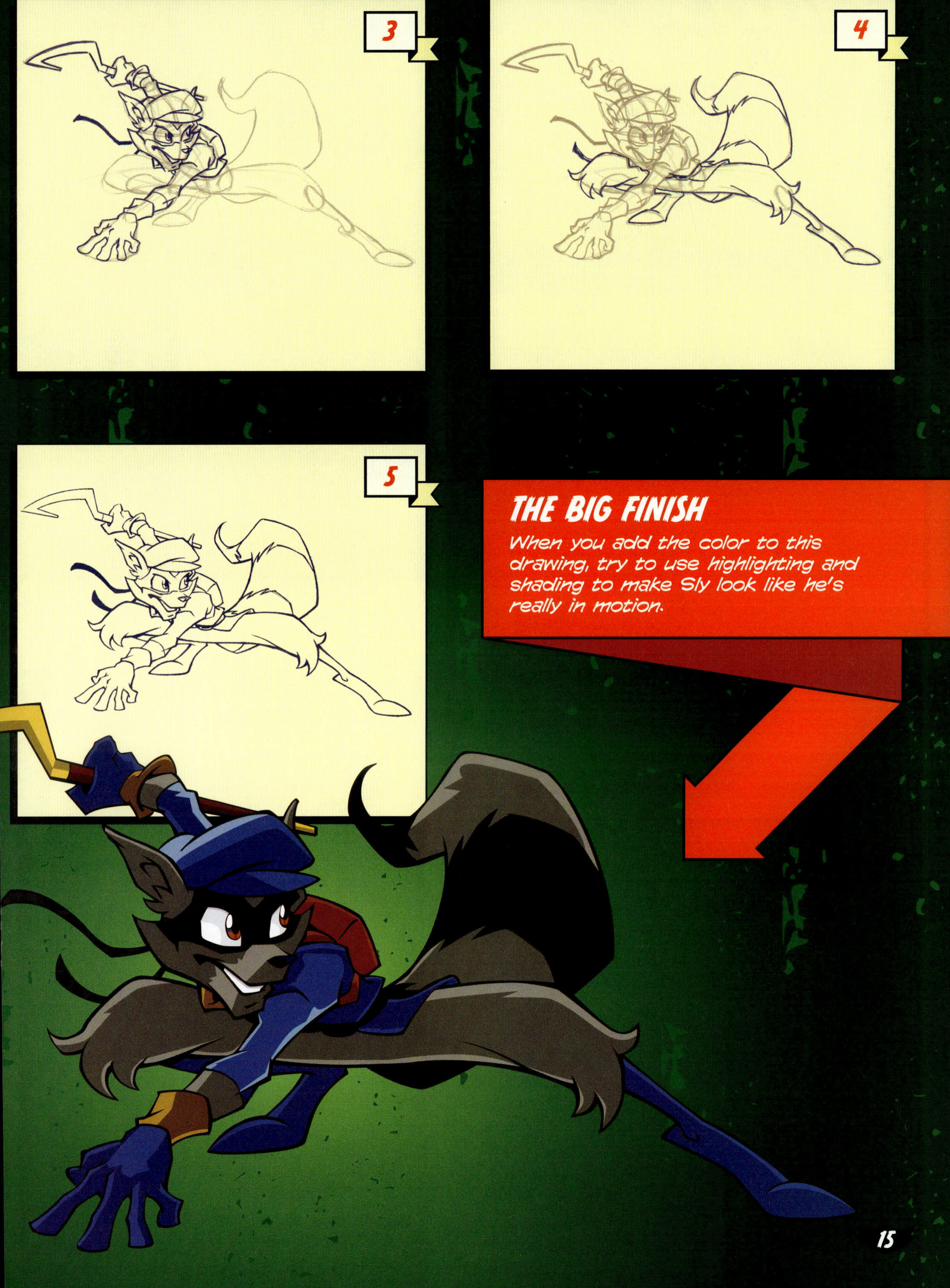

THE BIG FINISH

When you add the color to this drawing, try to use highlighting and shading to make Sly look like he's really in motion.

BENTLEY'S BLOWING HIS TOP!

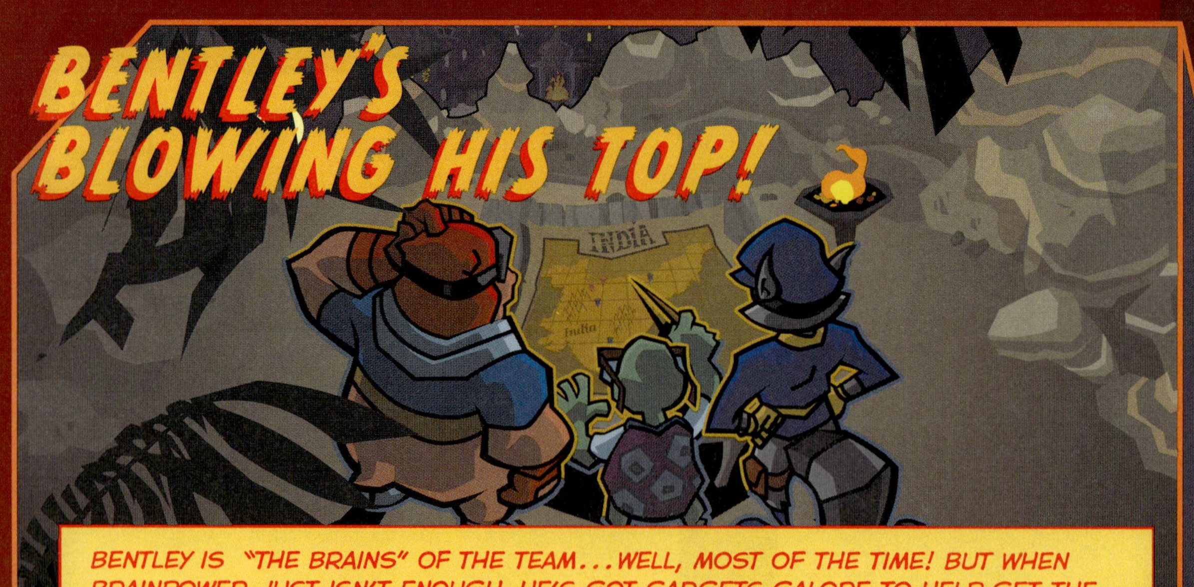

BENTLEY IS "THE BRAINS" OF THE TEAM . . . WELL, MOST OF THE TIME! BUT WHEN BRAINPOWER JUST ISN'T ENOUGH, HE'S GOT GADGETS GALORE TO HELP GET THE JOB DONE. THIS IS ONE OF THOSE TIMES WHEN BENTLEY'S PULLING OUT ALL THE STOPS—AND ALL THE DEVICES—IN ORDER TO HELP SLY ACCOMPLISH HIS MISSION.

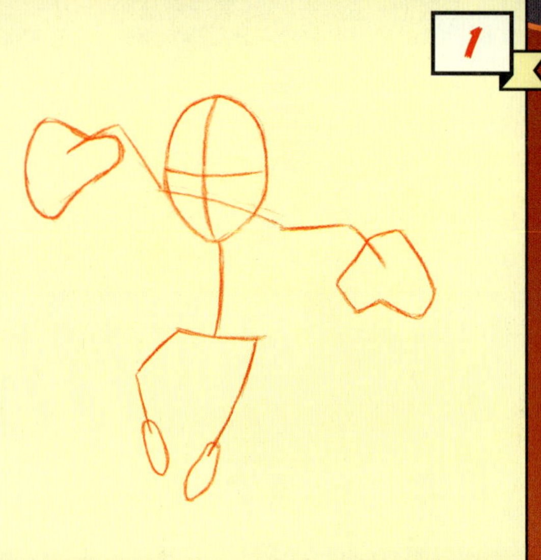

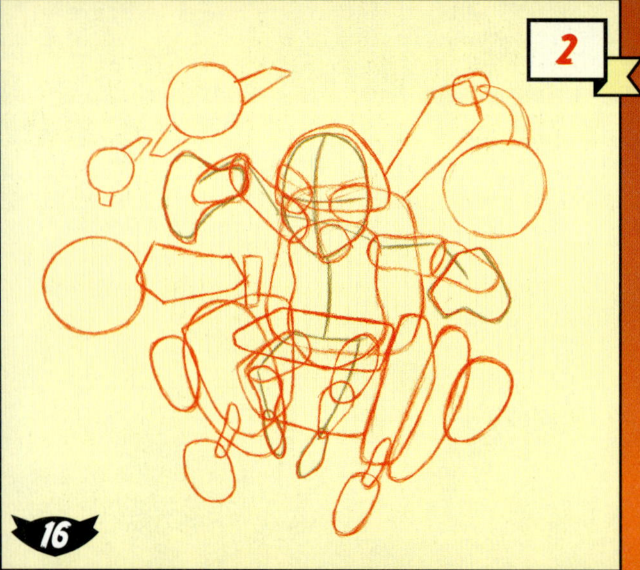

1. Start with the basic shapes. Draw a stick figure, then add the head, hands, and feet.

2. Use lots of circles to start filling in Bentley's body. Then add circles to create the basic shapes for the gadgets.

3. Gadgets galore! Add some details to each gadget, working on one at a time. Use squares and rectangles to shape Bentley's fingers. Then add details to his face and rocket chair.

4. Shape up Bentley's lower half, the wheels of his chair, and the rest of his gear. Don't forget the buttons on his laptop and the hinged springs that help give his devices some extra **zing!**

5. Strengthen the lines you want to keep and erase the rest. Add some fine details like the joints in Bentley's knees and feet.

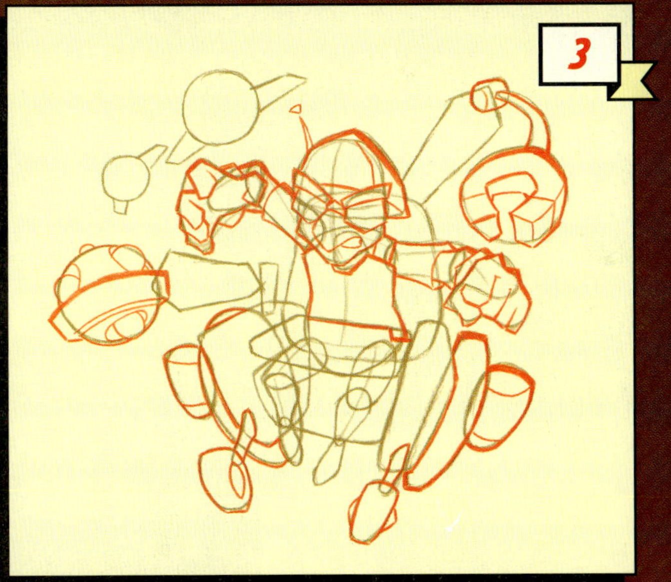

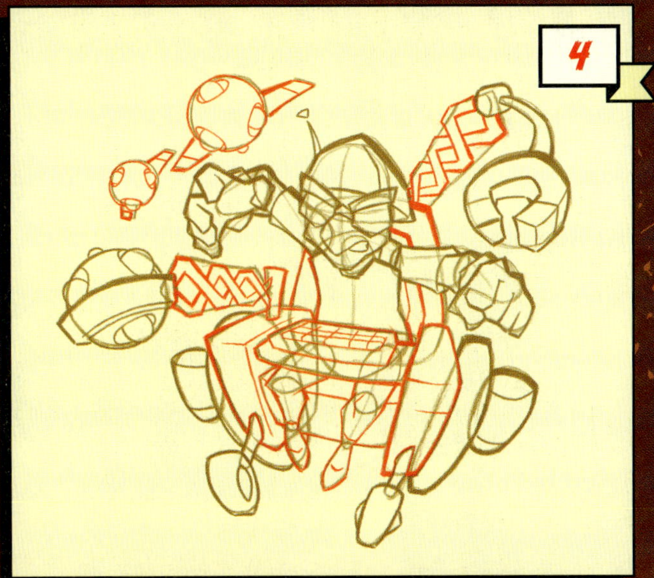

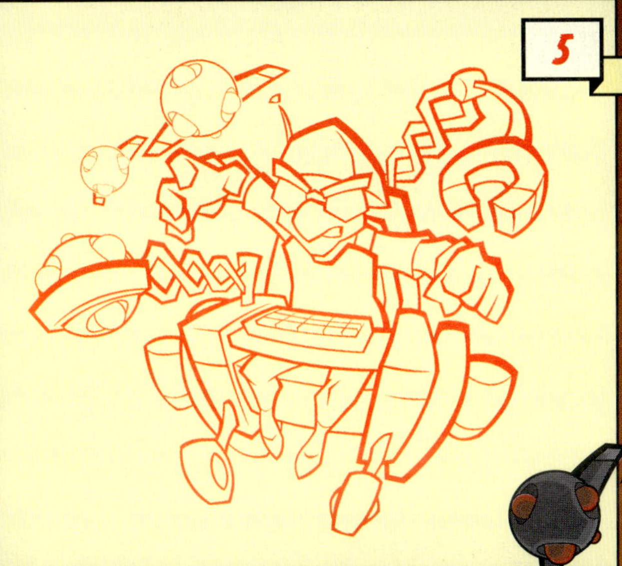

WORD FROM THE RACCOONUS

REMEMBER TO TAKE YOUR TIME THE FIRST TIME YOU TRY A NEW DRAWING!

THE BIG FINISH

Bring on the color! Check out the exhaust from those rockets! Use your imagination here—the flames don't have to be yellow. Try making them red, orange, or even blue. It's your drawing, so add your own details to personalize it and make it your own.

"THE MURRAY"

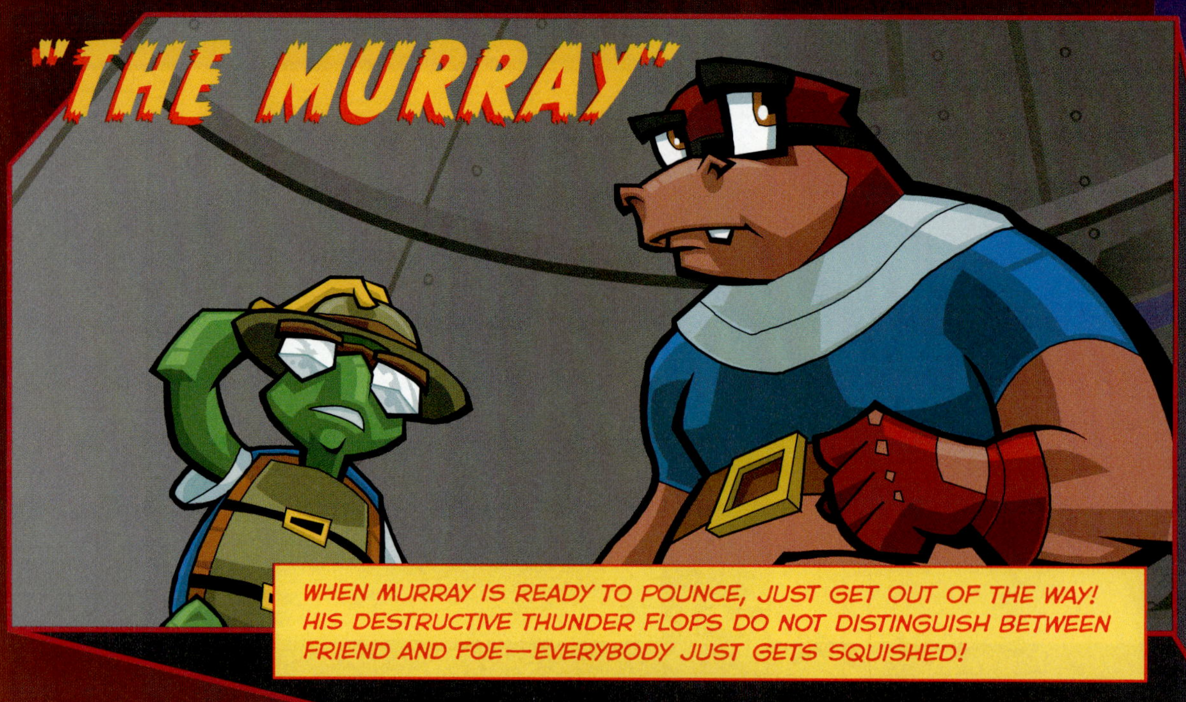

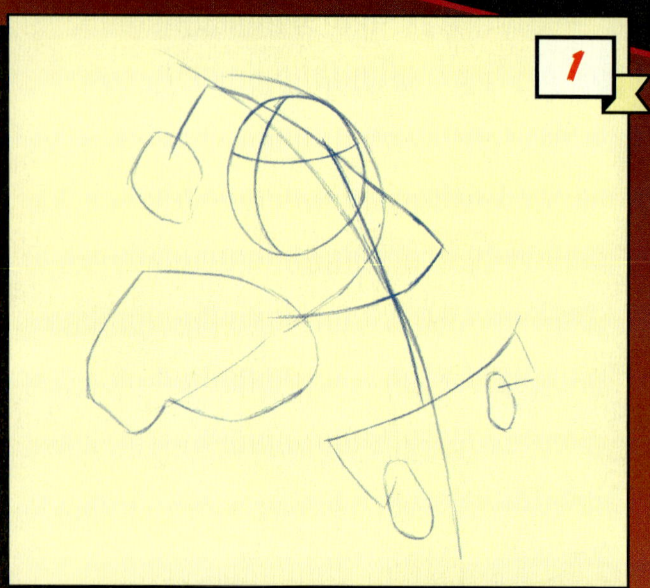

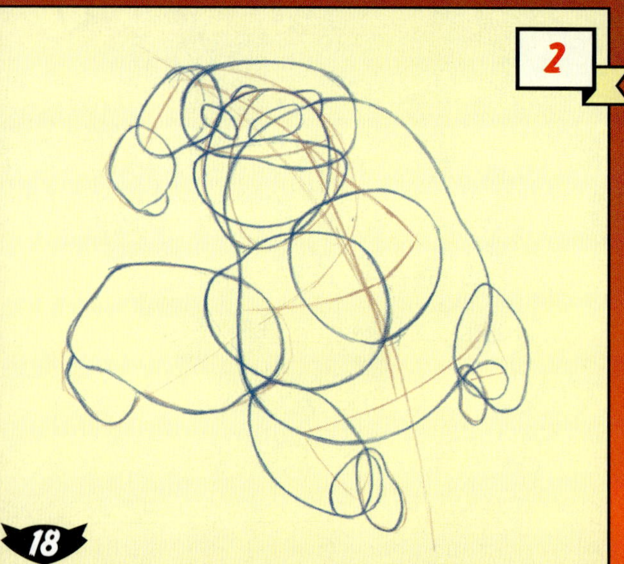

1. Begin with the basic shapes you practiced earlier. Include small ovals for Murray's right hand and feet. Draw a larger-shaped oval for Murray's left fist. **POW!**

2. This is where your drawing will start to come together! Murray's a big guy, so use BIG shapes to form his body. Add two large circles to create his extended left arm, and add some more circles and ovals to define his face.

3. Add details like Murray's eyebrows, fist, and knuckles. Because Murray is flexing his muscles in this pose, his left hand should be the same size as his head. Be sure to add the details to his gloves, and don't forget the scarf!

4. Murray's lower body doesn't have as much detail as the top, but at this point you'll want to add his belt buckle and belly button. Then add some sharper lines to define his legs.

5. Now you are ready to finalize your drawing. Trace over the light lines of your drawing with darker lines, focusing on details such as Murray's eyes, nostrils, tooth, and fists.

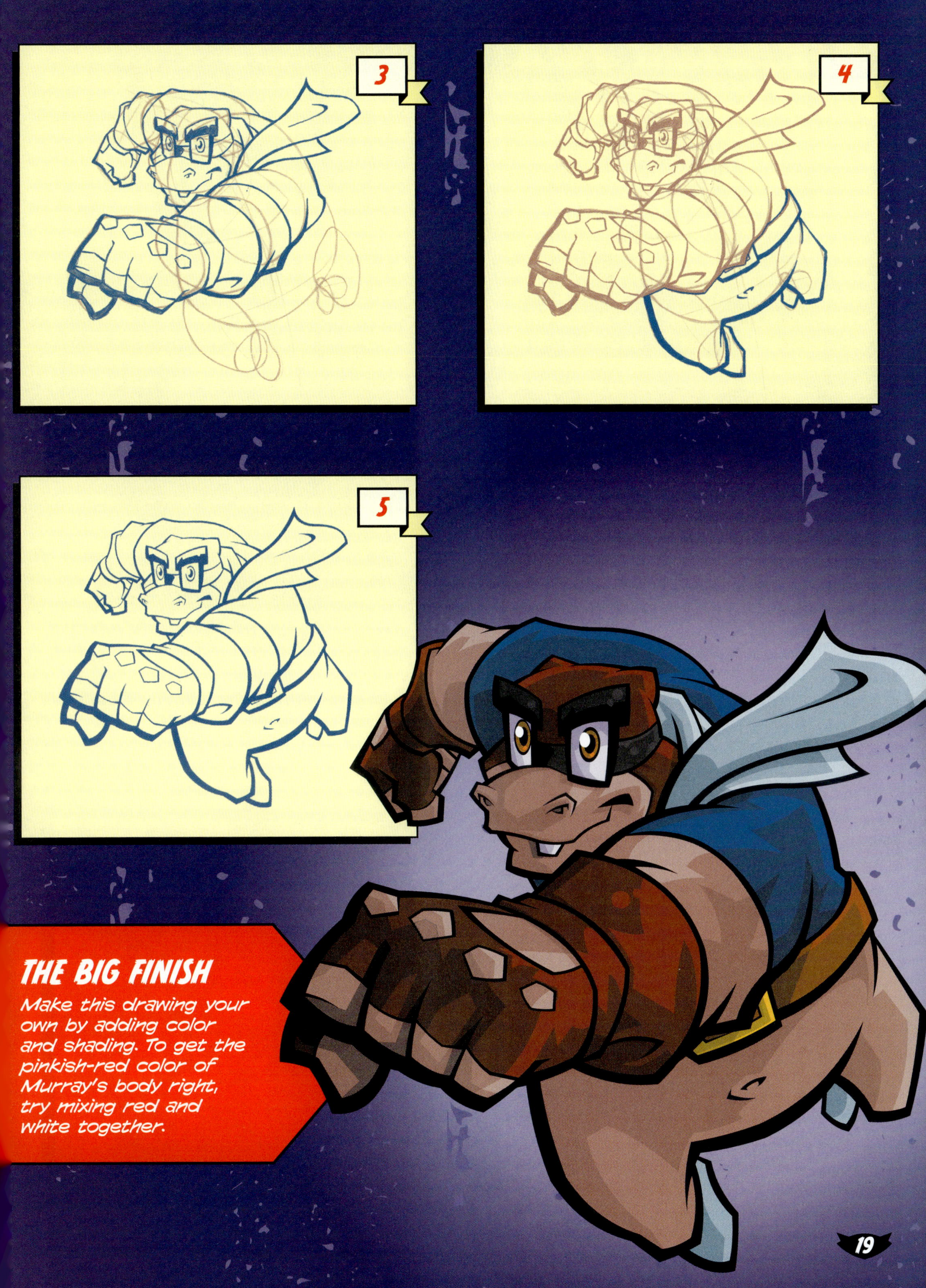

THE BIG FINISH

Make this drawing your own by adding color and shading. To get the pinkish-red color of Murray's body right, try mixing red and white together.

INSPECTOR FOX ON THE CASE

CARMELITA FOX IS AN HONEST AND HARDWORKING COP. BUT SOMETIMES SHE CAN GET A LITTLE ANGRY. IN THIS CASE IT'S BECAUSE THE RASCALLY RACCOON SLY COOPER HAS JUST SLIPPED THROUGH HER FINGERS—AGAIN.

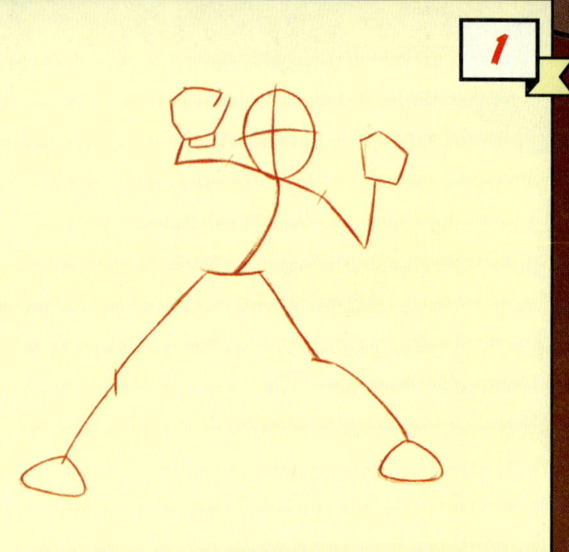

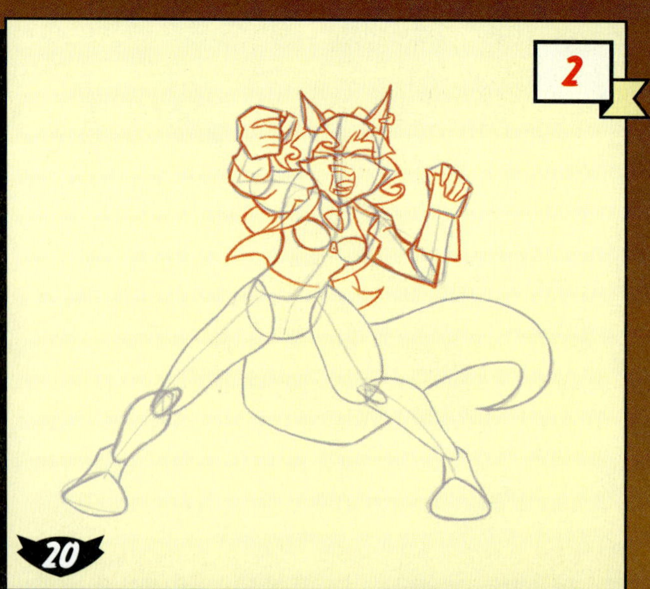

1. Begin with a stick figure as always. Make sure to give her a wide base—she's really ready for action here.
2. Use your basic shapes to create Carmelita's outline.
3. Add facial details as well as the outline for Carmelita's badge and uniform. Notice that Carmelita's eyes are closed in this drawing.
4. Go over her lower body now. Strengthen the lines of her tail and add details to those boots and her belt.
5. Trace over your lines and erase any stray traces from the earlier stages. This is your chance to add the fine details, such as her kneecaps and necklace.

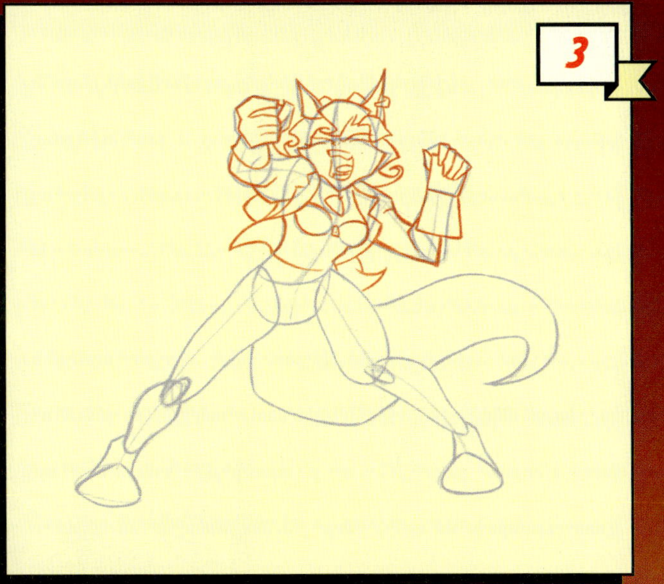

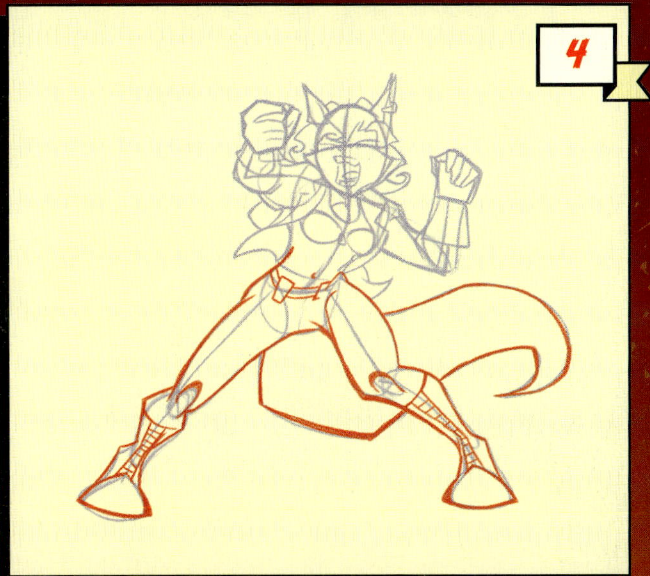

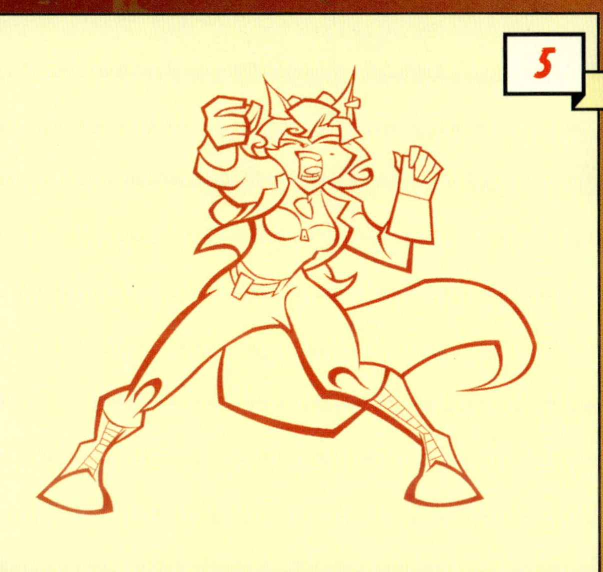

WORD FROM THE RACCOONUS

ADD AS MUCH OR AS LITTLE DETAIL AS YOU WANT—THE GOAL IS TO MAKE A DRAWING YOU ARE HAPPY WITH!

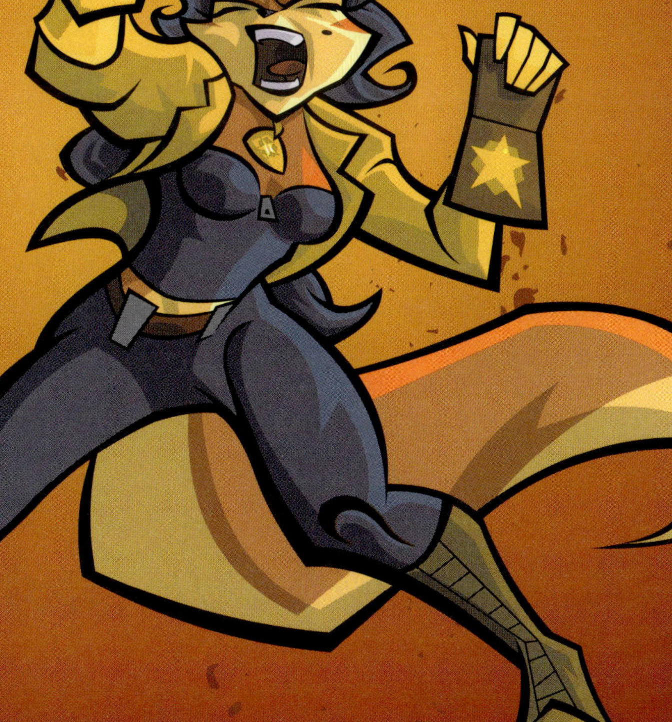

THE BIG FINISH

This is another drawing that gives you a chance to use some bright colors. Notice that Carmelita's hair and pants are the same color blue, and that her gloves match her badge.

MUGGSHOT

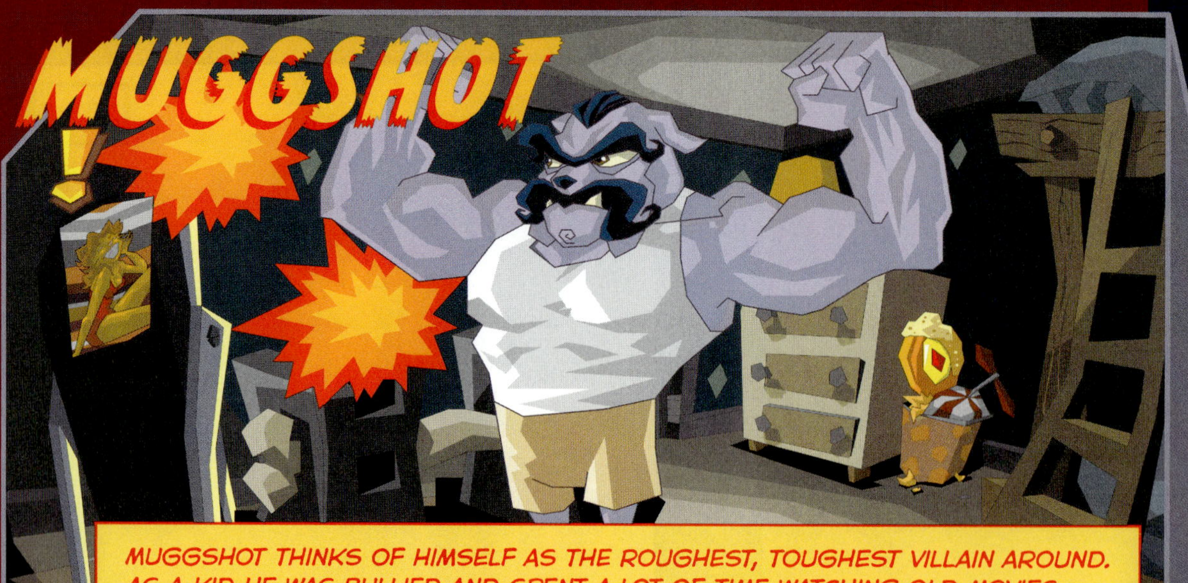

MUGGSHOT THINKS OF HIMSELF AS THE ROUGHEST, TOUGHEST VILLAIN AROUND. AS A KID HE WAS BULLIED AND SPENT A LOT OF TIME WATCHING OLD MOVIES. THOSE OLD-FASHIONED MOVIES INSPIRED HIM TO BECOME WHAT HE IS TODAY—THE MUSCLE-BOUND TOUGH GUY FOR THE FIENDISH FIVE!

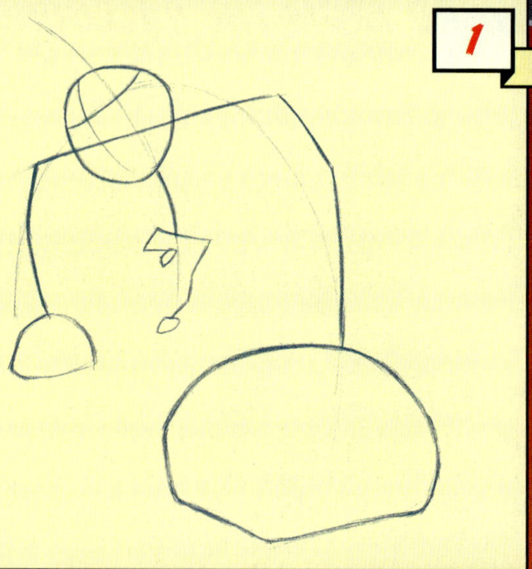

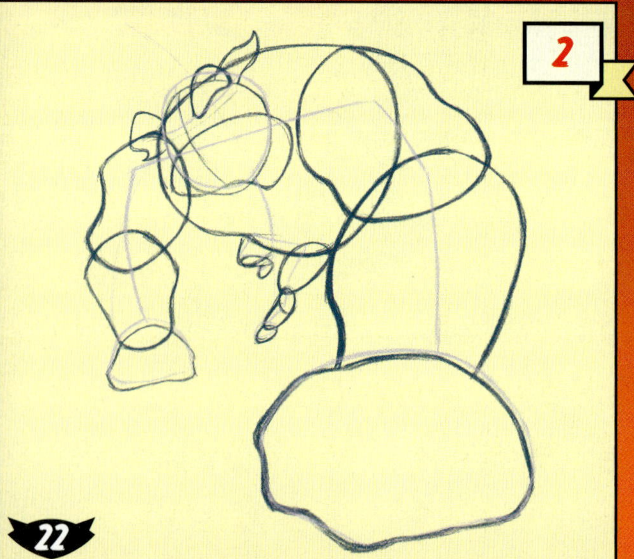

1. Start with a stick figure and a massive circle for Muggshot's fist. His legs and feet should be tiny in comparison.
2. Create his body with large basic shapes. His left arm is much larger and longer than his right. Take your time to get the proportions right.
3. Add the basic details. Muggshot has an intense look on his face, so spend some extra time working on facial details such as his curly moustache, gnarled teeth, and mean snarl. And don't overlook the spiked wrist cuffs—ouch!
4. The highlight here is on Muggshot's left hand. Notice that it looks larger than his entire lower body!
5. Smooth the drawing out by retracing the lines that work and erasing all the stray ones. Add extra lines to emphasize the muscles in both of Muggshot's big, burly arms.

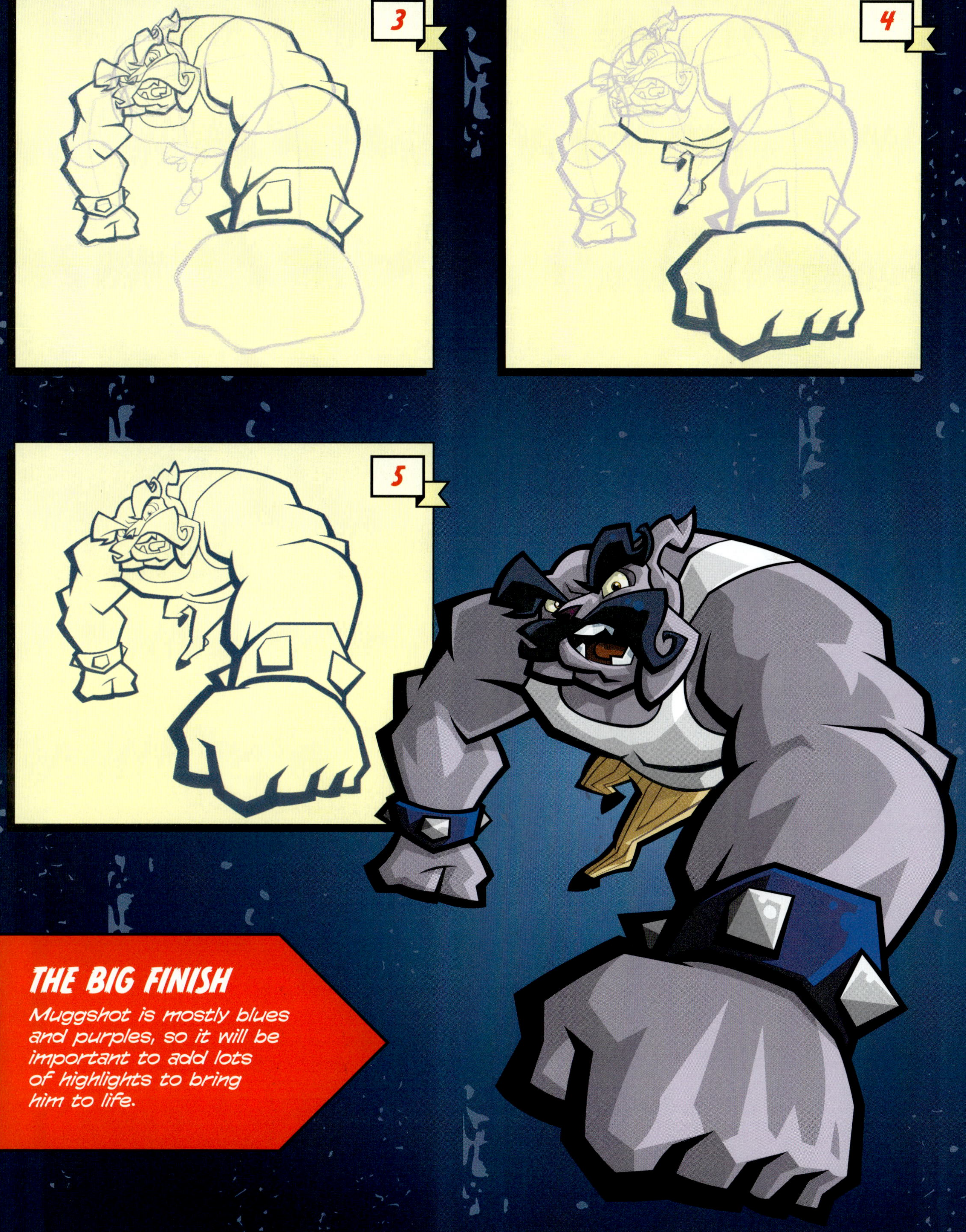

THE BIG FINISH

Muggshot is mostly blues and purples, so it will be important to add lots of highlights to bring him to life.

THE CONTESSA

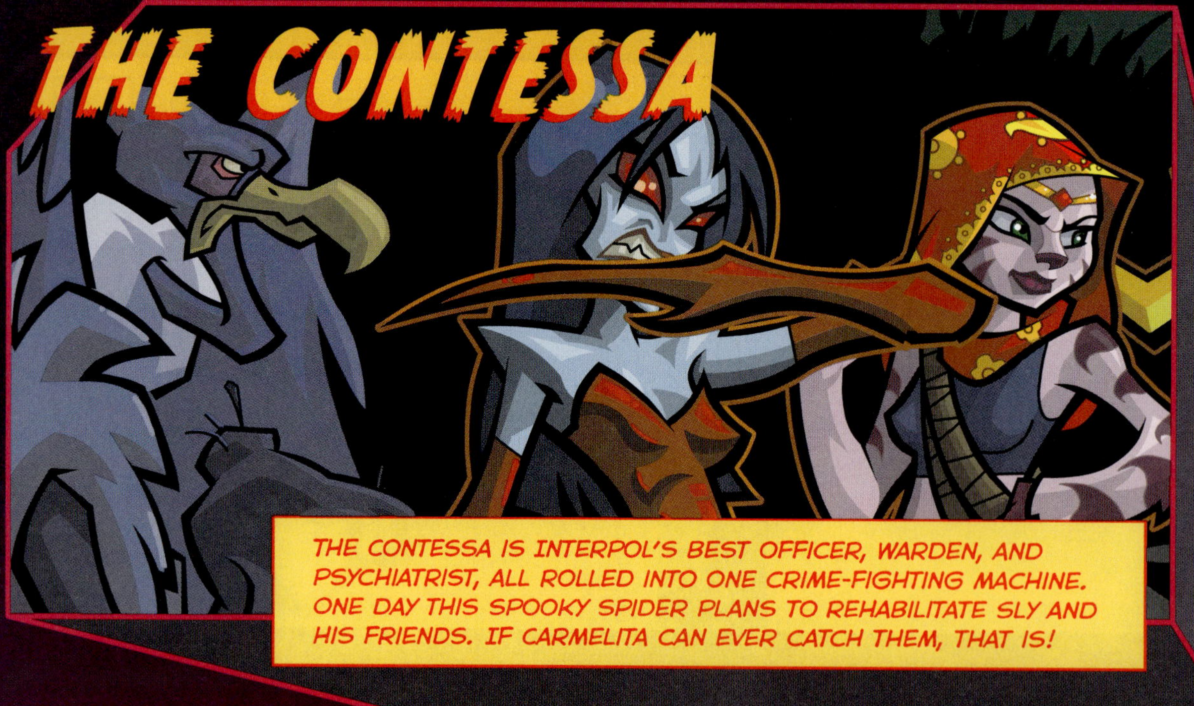

THE CONTESSA IS INTERPOL'S BEST OFFICER, WARDEN, AND PSYCHIATRIST, ALL ROLLED INTO ONE CRIME-FIGHTING MACHINE. ONE DAY THIS SPOOKY SPIDER PLANS TO REHABILITATE SLY AND HIS FRIENDS. IF CARMELITA CAN EVER CATCH THEM, THAT IS!

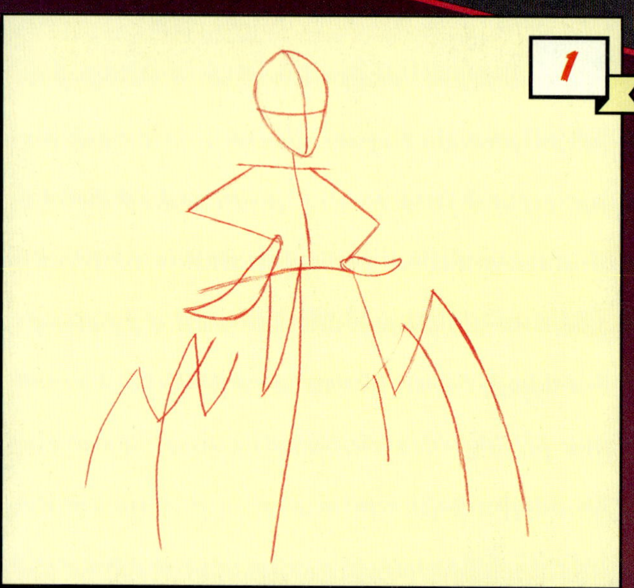

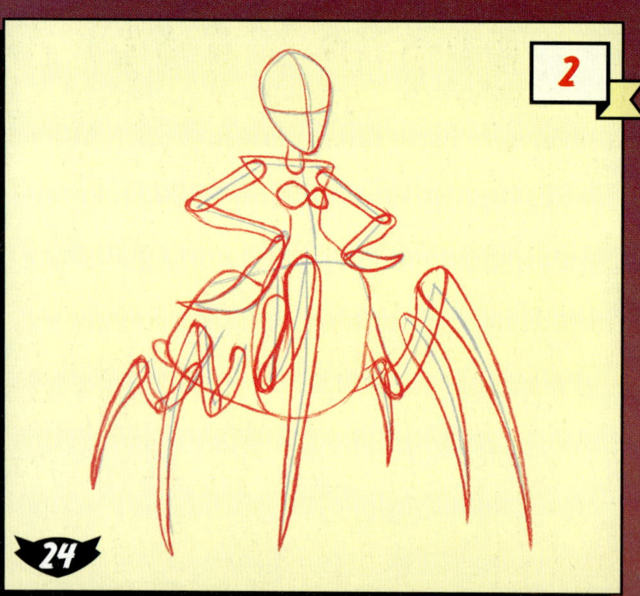

1. Remember to use light lines when you make the stick figure. You will have to erase these lines later on. Draw a cross over the Contessa's face. This will help you place her eyes and lips later on.

2. This is a fun character to draw. Use a big circle for her spider body. Each leg should taper to a point. Be sure to keep the proportions of her legs right.

3. Add detail to her upper body. Pay special attention to her face. Use the cross you drew in step 1 to place the ovals for her wide eyes and lips.

4. Finish adding details to her many legs. Try to make the ends look sharp by using razor-thin lines.

5. Refine your drawing by going over your picture and erasing the stray lines. Focus on the fine lines and details of the Contessa's scowling face.

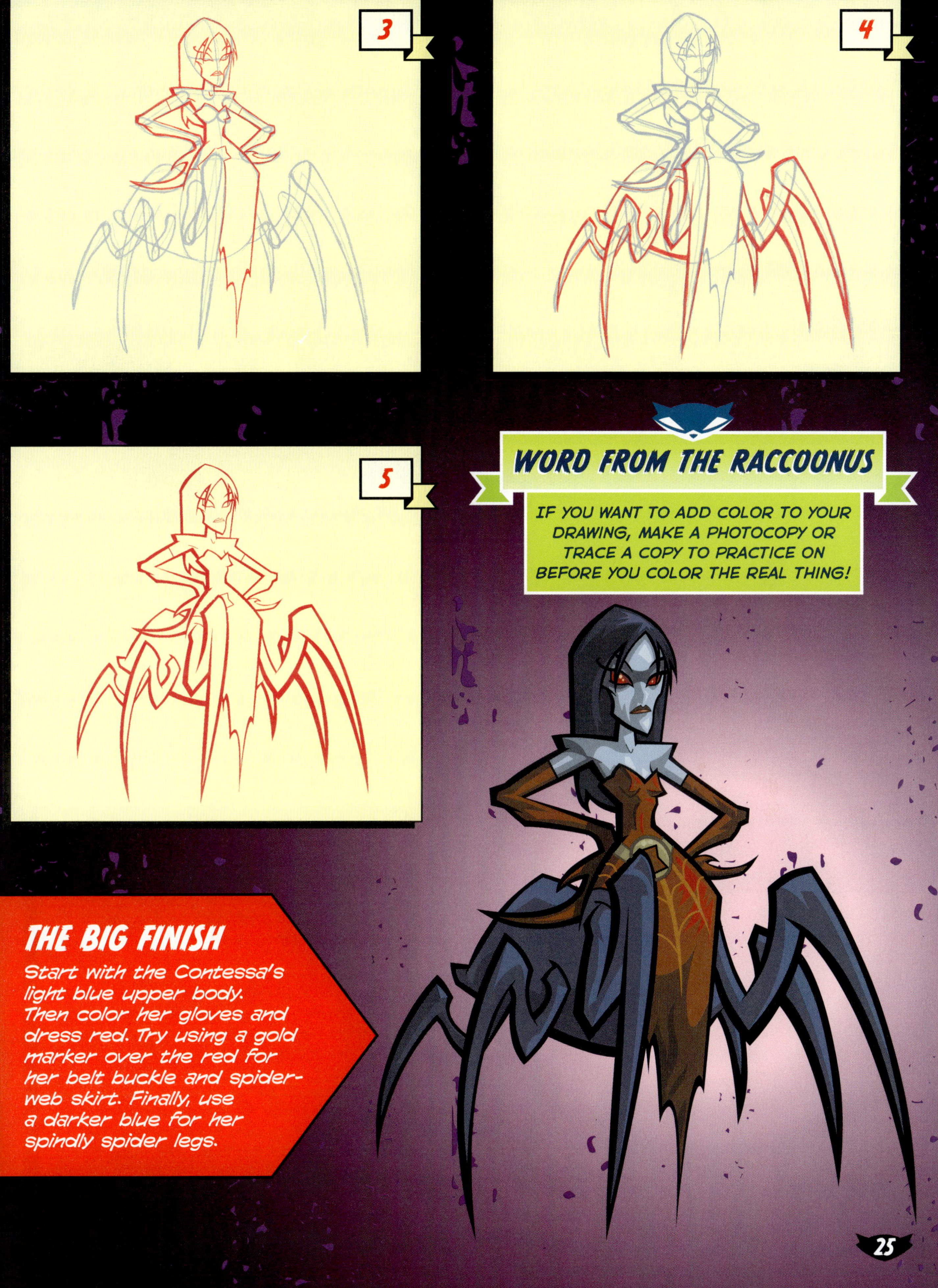

WORD FROM THE RACCOONUS

IF YOU WANT TO ADD COLOR TO YOUR DRAWING, MAKE A PHOTOCOPY OR TRACE A COPY TO PRACTICE ON BEFORE YOU COLOR THE REAL THING!

THE BIG FINISH

Start with the Contessa's light blue upper body. Then color her gloves and dress red. Try using a gold marker over the red for her belt buckle and spider-web skirt. Finally, use a darker blue for her spindly spider legs.

MZ. RUBY

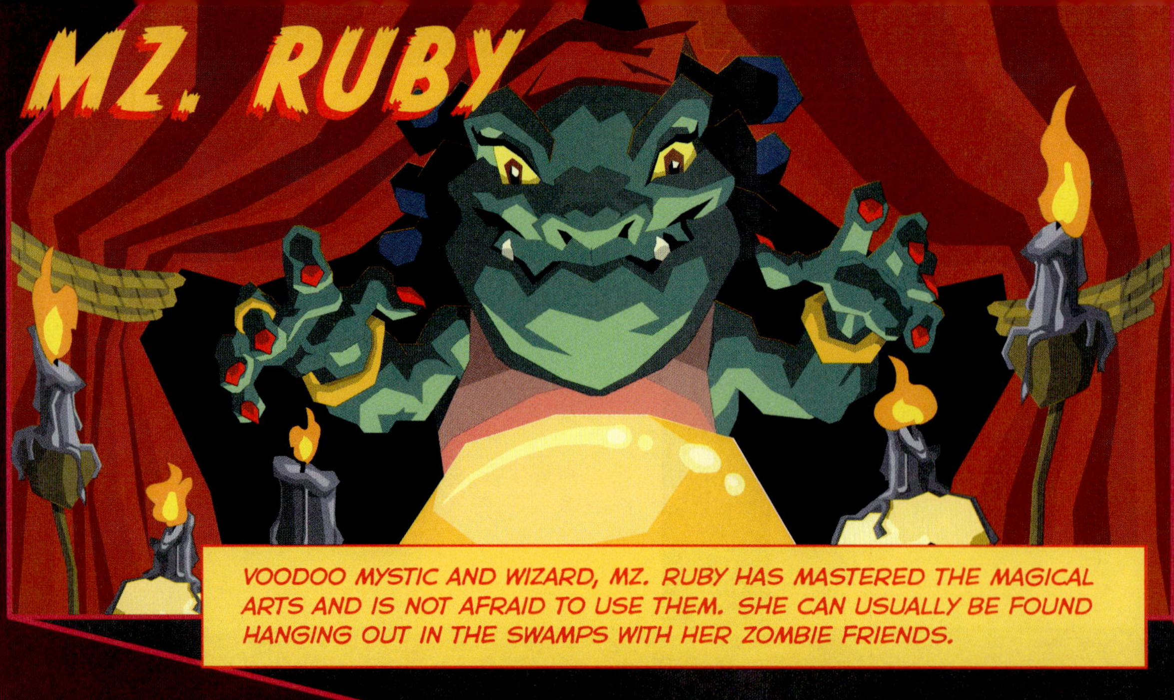

VOODOO MYSTIC AND WIZARD, MZ. RUBY HAS MASTERED THE MAGICAL ARTS AND IS NOT AFRAID TO USE THEM. SHE CAN USUALLY BE FOUND HANGING OUT IN THE SWAMPS WITH HER ZOMBIE FRIENDS.

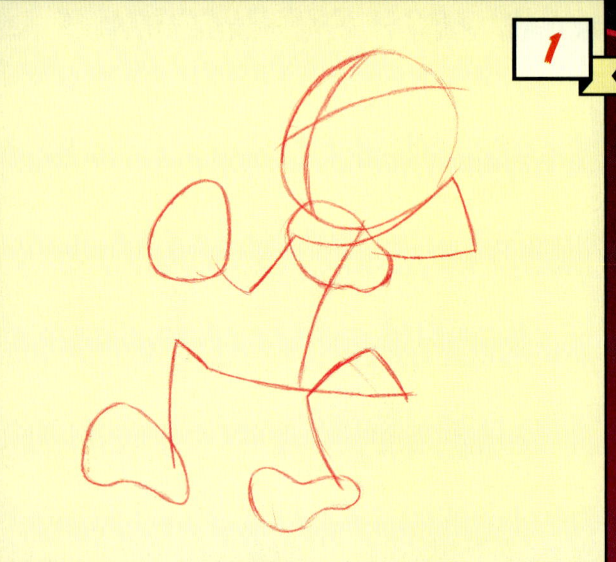

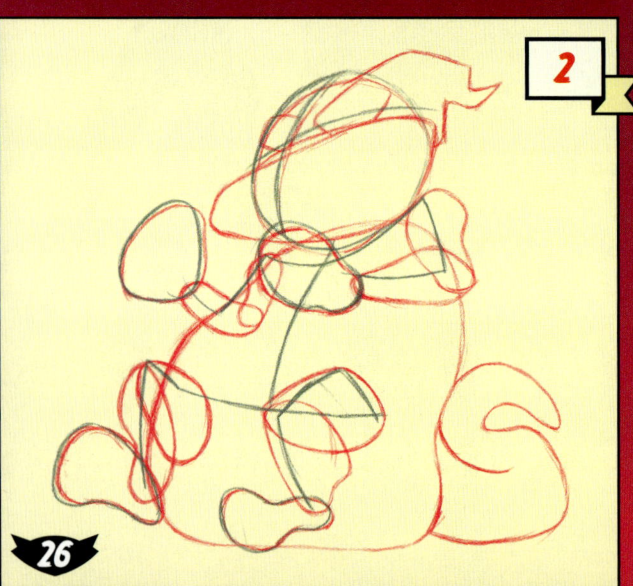

1 Mz. Ruby's stick figure makes it look like she'll be sneaking around, but she'll really be sitting. So leave some room below her feet to fill in her alligator body.

2 Start to shape Mz. Ruby by using the basic shapes for her body and limbs. Use ovals for her arms and legs, and an S-shaped squiggle for her tail.

3 Add some details to her face, hair, and hands. Use sharp lines for her jaw and jagged teeth, and then draw in her squinty eyes and long eyelashes. Draw squares and rectangles to form her bangle bracelets.

4 Add the spike to her tail and then focus on the feet. Detailing the legs and claws can be a little tough, so take your time with it.

5 Time to bring it all together. Once you have erased the lines you don't want, go back and work on the fine details. The claws, eyes, and teeth all deserve a little extra attention!

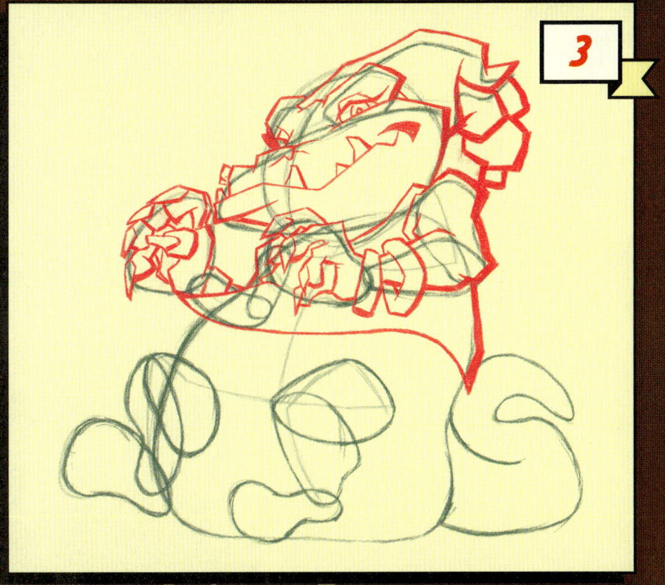

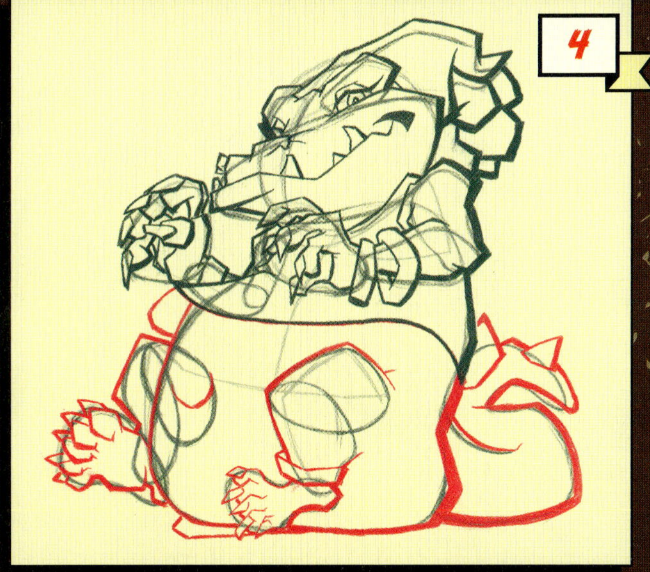

5

WORD FROM THE RACCOONUS

DON'T TRY TO BE PERFECT! SOMETIMES "MISTAKES" HELP LEAD TO THE BEST DRAWINGS. REMEMBER, IF YOU DON'T LIKE YOUR DRAWING, YOU CAN ALWAYS ERASE LINES OR BEGIN AGAIN.

THE BIG FINISH

This gator is green all over! Start with a lighter green, and then use a darker green on Mz. Ruby's legs and arms. The whiter the teeth, the scarier they'll look! And don't forget the bits of red detail, such as her fingernails, head scarf, and the ruby in her belly button.

JEAN-BISON

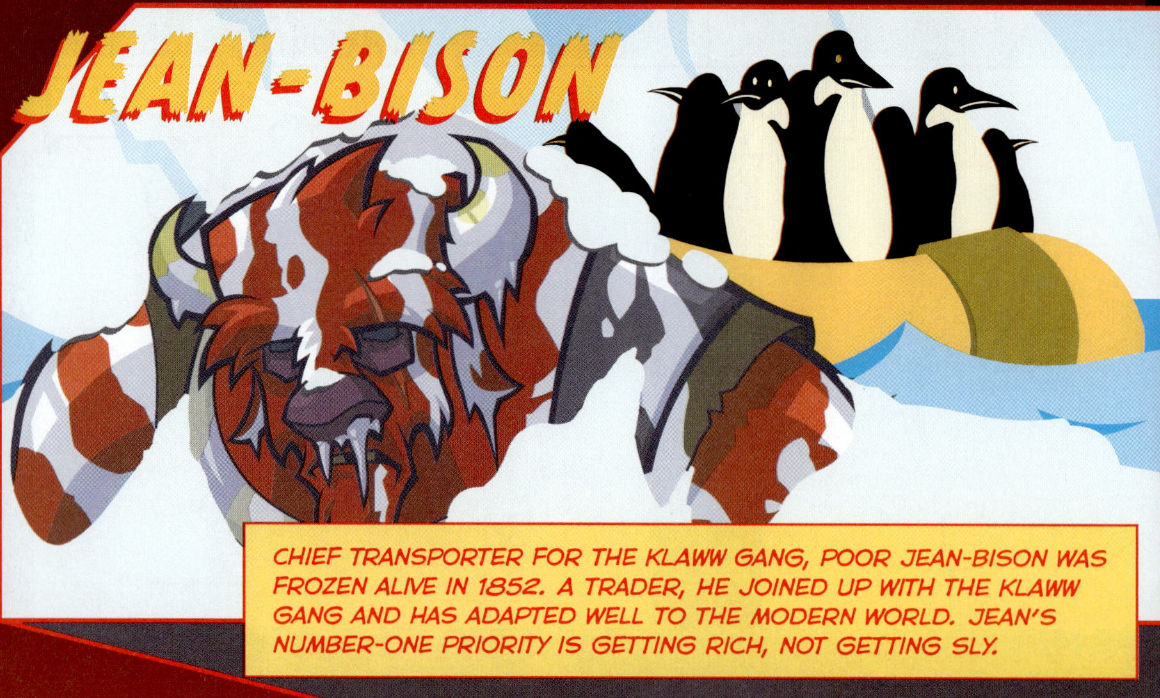

CHIEF TRANSPORTER FOR THE KLAWW GANG, POOR JEAN-BISON WAS FROZEN ALIVE IN 1852. A TRADER, HE JOINED UP WITH THE KLAWW GANG AND HAS ADAPTED WELL TO THE MODERN WORLD. JEAN'S NUMBER-ONE PRIORITY IS GETTING RICH, NOT GETTING SLY.

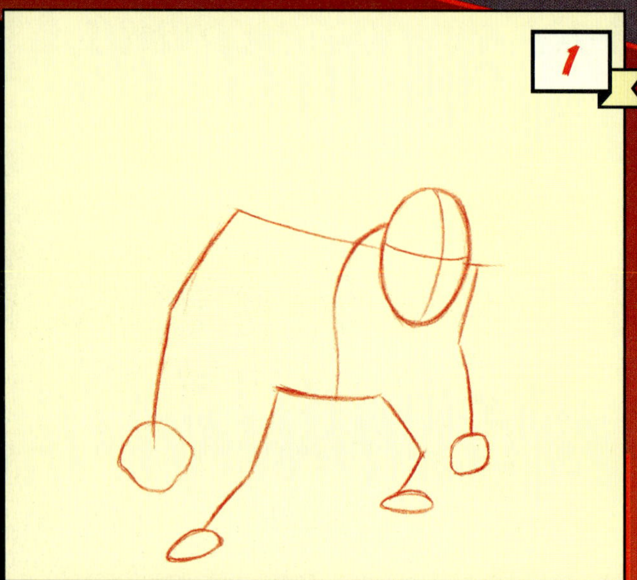

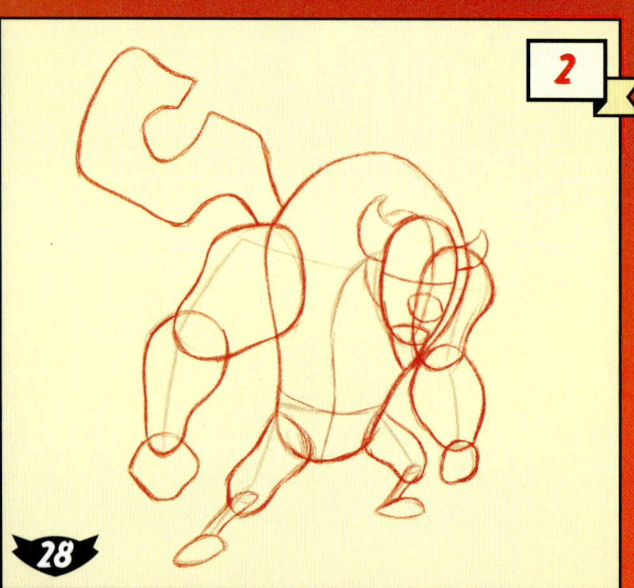

1. Start by creating a stick figure with broad shoulders and a wide stance. Use a slightly pointy oval for his head and hooves.

2. Create the basic shape of your drawing. To create Jean-Bison's club, try drawing a square, then drawing a semicircle on one side of it.

3. Create the first layer of detail by filling in his face and gloves. Jean's hunched back should have a jagged edge to emphasize his matted fur. Then add Jean's harness, wrist wraps, and horns.

4. Jean-Bison's club has lots of detail, so start there. Add the bands and whatever lines you'd like to simulate a real wooden club. Then move on to his lower half. Jean's a little bit rough around the edges, so be sure to use lots of jagged lines.

5. Add more details if you want and trace over the light lines with darker ones. If you haven't already added the amulet around his waist, draw it in now. And make sure you have those tiny details such as his teeth and nose taken care of!

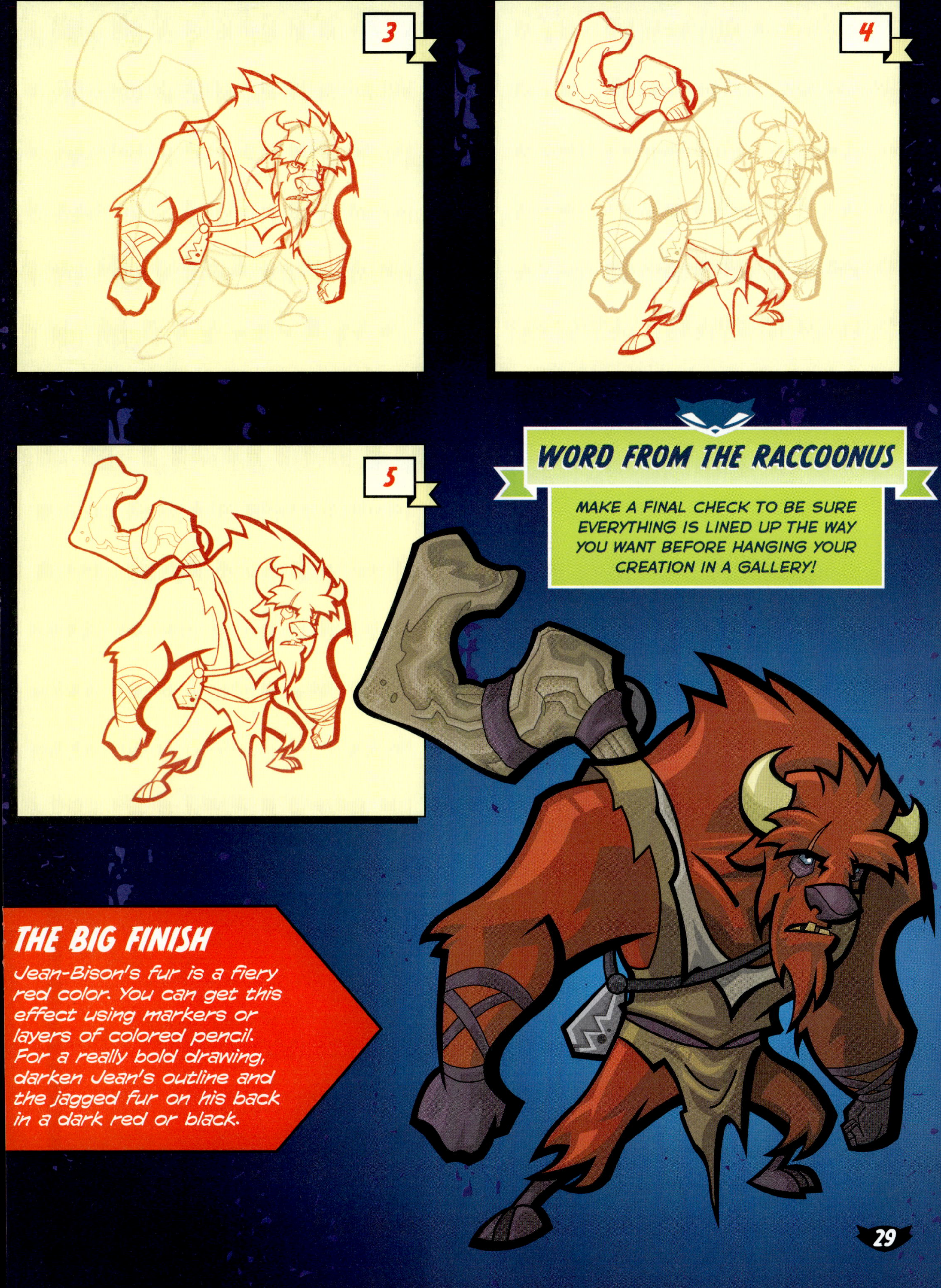

WORD FROM THE RACCOONUS

MAKE A FINAL CHECK TO BE SURE EVERYTHING IS LINED UP THE WAY YOU WANT BEFORE HANGING YOUR CREATION IN A GALLERY!

THE BIG FINISH

Jean-Bison's fur is a fiery red color. You can get this effect using markers or layers of colored pencil. For a really bold drawing, darken Jean's outline and the jagged fur on his back in a dark red or black.

LEFWEE

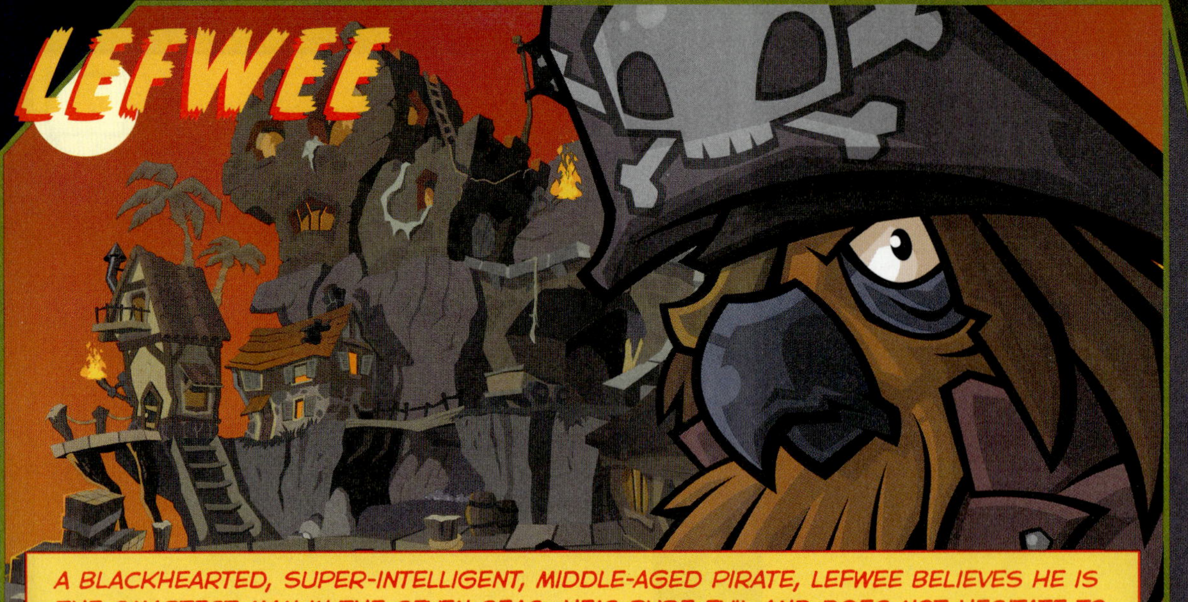

A BLACKHEARTED, SUPER-INTELLIGENT, MIDDLE-AGED PIRATE, LEFWEE BELIEVES HE IS THE SMARTEST MAN IN THE SEVEN SEAS. HE'S PURE EVIL AND DOES NOT HESITATE TO SHOW HIS HATRED TOWARD ANYONE WHO GETS IN HIS WAY, INCLUDING HIS OWN MEN.

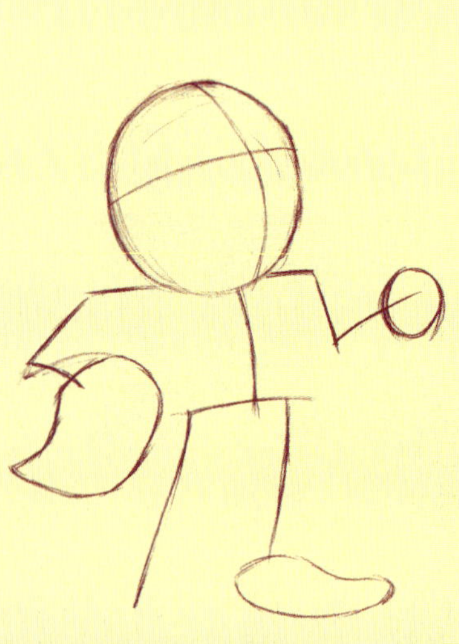

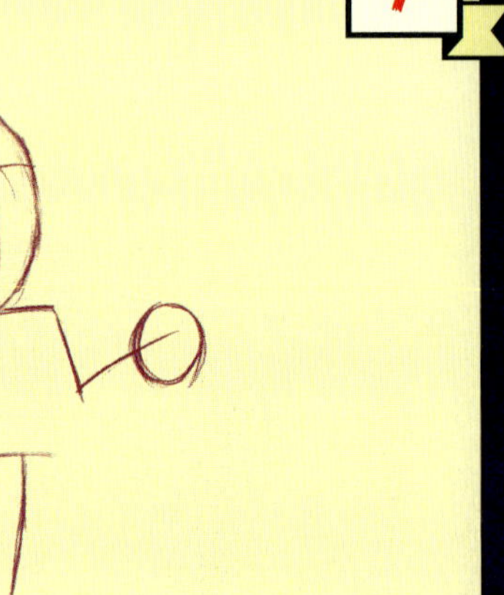

1

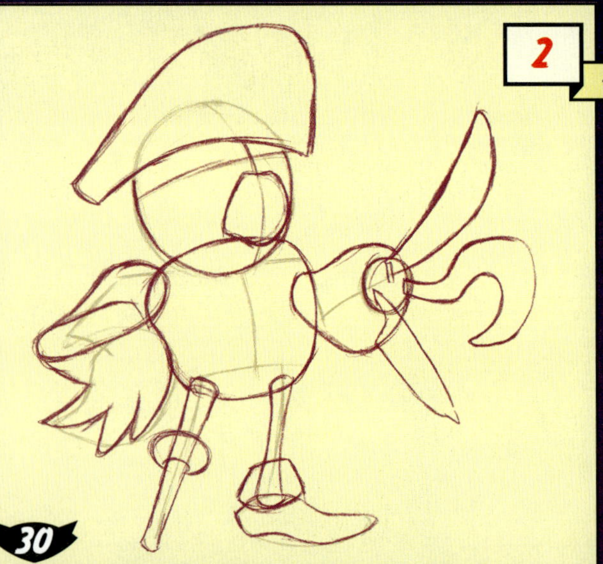

2

1. This guy is smaller than the other drawings you've done, so start with a little stick figure and a large circle for his head.
2. Notice that LeFwee's body is only as large as his head. Use long, thin rectangles to form his legs. Then add elongated ovals for his knife and screw gadgets, and semicircles for his hook.
3. Use triangles to define LeFwee's feathery right hand and sharp, pointed beak. Don't forget that his beard of feathers is going to cover his shirt, so you can make those lines nice and heavy. This is a great time to lightly pencil in small details such as the buttons on his shirt and sleeves.
4. Add some dimension to LeFwee's peg leg. Then use rectangles to finish the lines at the bottom of his coat—it's an easy detail to miss if you don't look closely.
5. Erase the stray lines and strengthen the lines you want to keep.

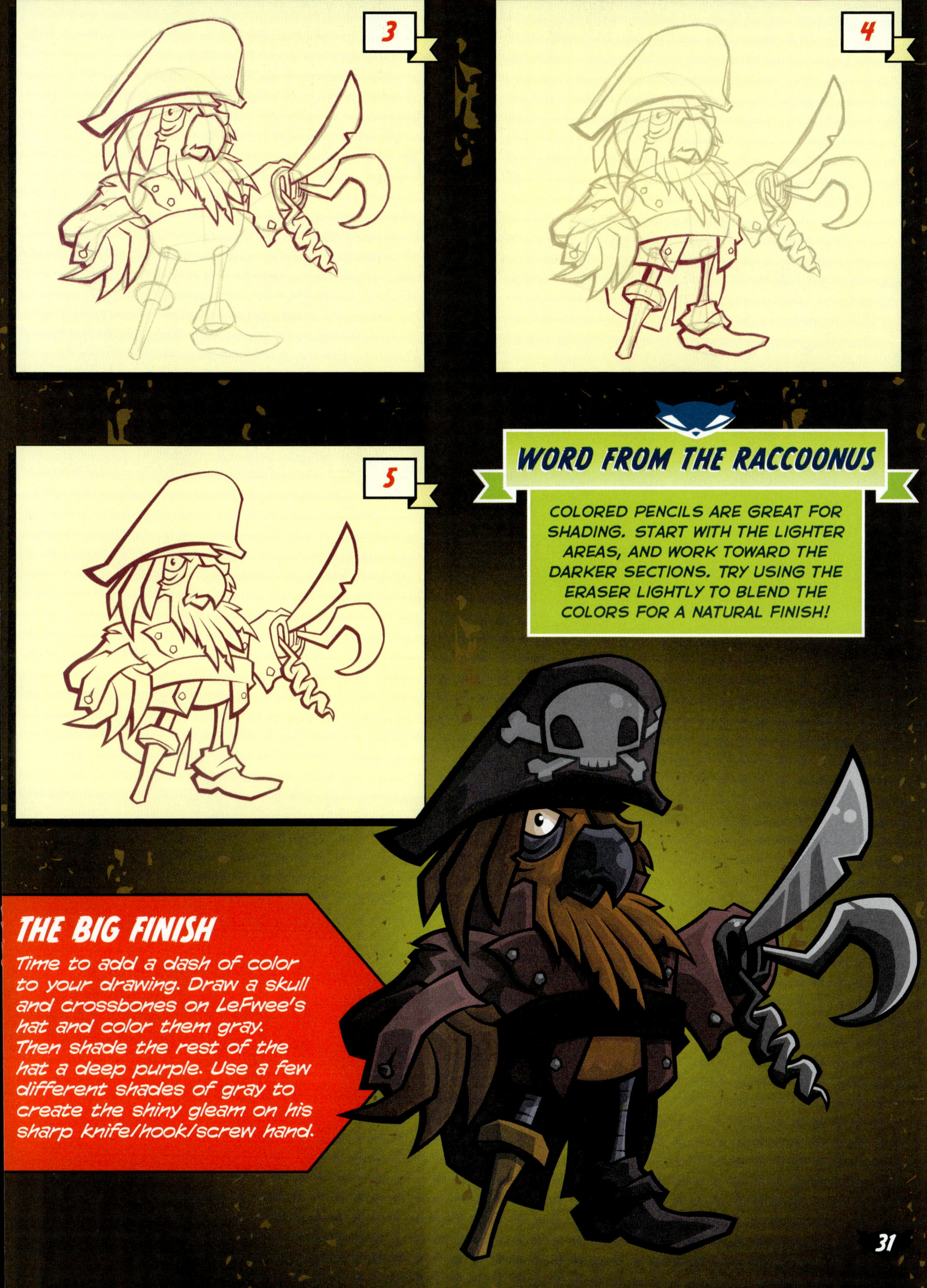
3
4
5
WORD FROM THE RACCOONUS
COLORED PENCILS ARE GREAT FOR SHADING. START WITH THE LIGHTER AREAS, AND WORK TOWARD THE DARKER SECTIONS. TRY USING THE ERASER LIGHTLY TO BLEND THE COLORS FOR A NATURAL FINISH!
THE BIG FINISH
Time to add a dash of color to your drawing. Draw a skull and crossbones on LeFwee's hat and color them gray. Then shade the rest of the hat a deep purple. Use a few different shades of gray to create the shiny gleam on his sharp knife/hook/screw hand.

CONGRATULATIONS!

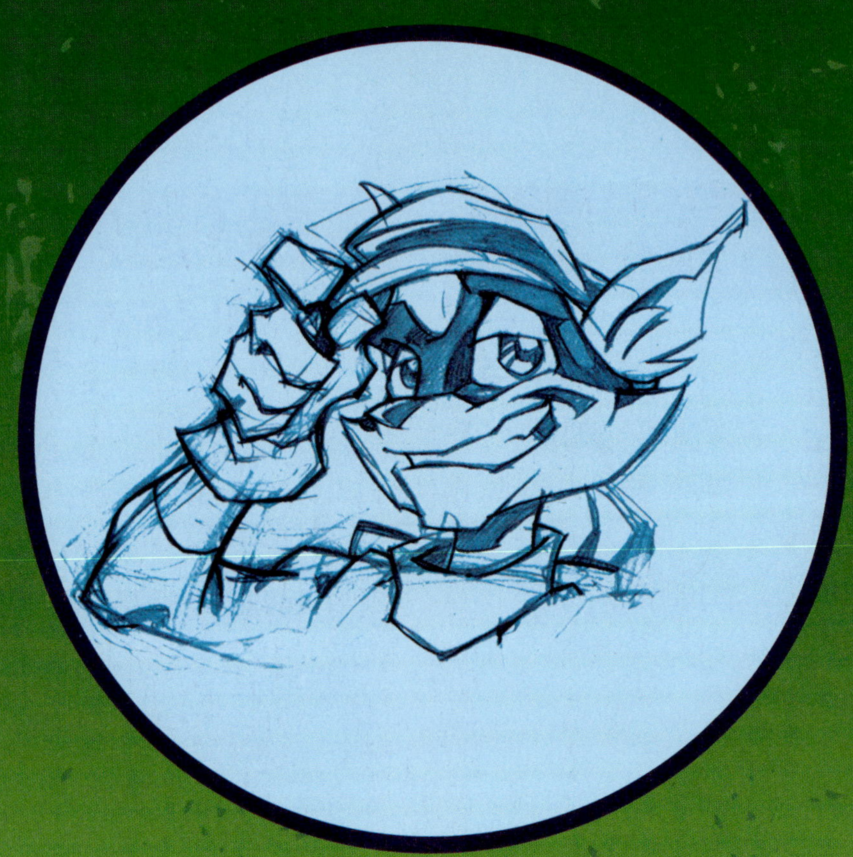

YOU HAVE LEARNED TO DRAW SLY COOPER, HIS FRIENDS, AND HIS ENEMIES, AND YOU'RE WELL ON YOUR WAY TO BECOMING AN ARTIST. WITH A LITTLE BIT OF PRACTICE, YOU JUST MAY CREATE DRAWINGS GOOD ENOUGH TO DRAW THE ATTENTION OF THE MASTER THIEF SLY HIMSELF. GREAT JOB!